Pru Goes Troppo

Stevan Treleaven Eldred-Grigg is an award-winning novelist and historian. He was born in the Grey Valley, New Zealand in 1952 and grew up in the small mining town of Blackball and the suburbs of Christchurch. He graduated from the University of Canterbury in 1975 with an MA in history before obtaining a PhD at the Australian National University in Canberra in 1978.

by Stevan Eldred-Grigg

Fiction & Autofiction

Green Grey Rain
My History, I Think
Oracles & Miracles & Zombies (with Helen Mae Innes)
Bangs
Shanghai Boy
Sheng Xian Qu Ji
Kaput!
Blue Blood
Mum
Gardens of Fire
The Shining City
The Siren Celia
Oracles and Miracles

Non-Fiction

Phoney Wars (with Hugh Eldred-Grigg)
White Ghosts, Yellow Peril (with Zeng Dazheng)
People, People, People
The Great Wrong War
Diggers, Hatters and Whores
Xin Xilan de Wenxue Lucheng
The Rich: a New Zealand History
New Zealand Working People
Pleasures of the Flesh
A New History of Canterbury
A Southern Gentry

Pru Goes Troppo

STEVAN ELDRED-GRIGG

Piwaiwaka Press

Published by Piwaiwaka Press
Copyright © Stevan Eldred-Grigg 2020
First published 2020. Reprinted 2021, 2023.

Front cover artwork: Garland by Sandra Thomson.
Cover design: Amanda Sutcliffe

ISBN 978-0-473-53875-0 (softcover)
ISBN 978-0-473-53876-7 (epub)
ISBN 978-0-473-54058-6 (kindle)

Part 1: CHAPTER ONE

'The sweeping gravel driveway curving, um, beautifully through the autumnal woodlands of, um, the serene autumnal woodlands of the Beauchamp Estate,' I'm dictating into my phone while swinging the wheel of my wee car, 'make you think you've been beamed back two hundred years to the days of Jane Austen.'

I'm laying it on with a trowel because it's my job.

What do I really want to say?

Money, that's what I want to say. Loot. Old loot. Lots of old loot. Pissloads of ancestral pelf slithering down the generations and buying by the swag the skills of architects, builders, landscapers, gardeners, housekeepers, grooms – and, right now, one loser of a journo.

'Baaaa,' says some sheep somewhere.

'Emma Woodhouse or Elizabeth Bennet would love to wander, um, stroll – saunter? – into this lovely long house of creamy stone with classic proportions – um, neoclassical proportions – '

A lady in jeans and a cashmere sweater steps out into a colonnaded portico. Must have heard the hissing of gravel under the wheels of my little Nissan. The lady's not tall. A bit plump. Nice tits. Her hair is in a bob, ash blonde. She's fifty or so, according to our files back at the mag.

My age, in other words.

Not a good age.

'A parterre, formal yet welcoming, um, inviting, with clusters of terracotta urns and a reflecting pond, and behind the parterre another autumnal expanse of, er, sylvan woodlands.'

What else would woodlands be but sylvan, you might ask. I'm fighting against my nerves when I come to these sorts of places. These sorts of places aren't the sorts of places you expect to find people like me. You know, people who don't have old money. People who don't have new money. People who don't have any sort of money except not enough money. People with the wrong whakapapa. I don't fit in. I won't fit in. I stick out like some numb dumb sore thumb and the stocky little lady on the portico – quite pretty, actually – she knows, and – and, well, I've got to watch myself not to say something waspish.

Why did I suggest to the editor that we do this series of spreads?

New Old Landed Estates of Canterbury, that's what we're calling the spreads. The angle is new country houses that people a century or so from now will see as part of the province's heritage of stately homes, sort of thing. Our photographer will come another day. The mag is glossy and sells mostly to women in the suburbs. Women who've got a few spare bucks. A few, but not a lot of, spare bucks. Women, poor saps, who'll max out the credit card to buy what the ads in the mag are hyping, trying to kid themselves that by buying they're inching a notch or two upwards –

Women trying to kid themselves they can copy this lady in the cashmere and the ash blonde bob.

Our readers know next to nothing about these people and their aloof way of doing things. A lot never even knew the snoots existed till we started the spreads. Our covert editorial angle, below the sugary sweetness of the surface sycophancy, is political. We're hoping to give a few readers a bit of a wake up, make them ask themselves why some people are so loaded when most are loadless. You know, raise political consciousness.

A revolution on the way, comrades!

Right, well worth a try – or at least kidding ourselves it's worth a try – and what the hell, it's a job, and these days jobs in journalism, thanks to the internet –

'Hi,' she says, stepping forward, holding out her right hand as I stumble towards her after bumbling out of the Nissan. 'You must be Wayne.'

'Dwayne,' I mumble. 'Mrs Blandwood?'

'Pru,' she says, giving my prole paw a good dry shake.

'Sure, er, Pru,' says me, grimacing, twisting my face into a professional smile, also part of my job. I catch her giving a quick glance down at my legs. Hah! My gears are totally wrong for this sort of outing. Black. Cheap. Cheap gears are what I like, they let me kid myself I'm sticking to my guns, staying true to who I am, what I am – whatever that is – which is sort of cool because I know that seen through her eyes I'm just some sad try-hard staring down the gun at late middle age yet kidding himself he can sport the new emo look and wear his black hair long and swept across his eyes, and cram his legs

and bum into tight black jeans, jeans that are tight as
– they're the latest look, they call them *skinny*.

Mrs Blandwood – oops, Pru – is smiling, a smile
as professional as mine, since while my profession is
journo her profession is lady bountiful.

Or is her smile – something else? The glance –
the look she shot down at my tight pants.

Fuck! The squiress was checking out my tackle!
Or was she?

I peek at her face, the skin of which is a soft pink,
very soft. A quiet little string of pearls around her
neck. A quiet little pearl in the lobe of each ear. She
keeps smiling, though the smile's only on the lips,
not in the eyes.

'Shall we go this way?' she says.

The mansion, when we get inside, is just what
you expect. Fucking gorgeous! Not that I can say that
in the mag. The mag wants anodyne words. Gracious.
Spacious. Quietly echoing. Antiques. Luxury.

Class.

A woman who seems to be some sort of servant
gives a nod. A man who seems to be some sort of
servant brings in an armful of firewood. Blue gum.
Big fragrant hunks. Pru shows me both storeys and
tells me the story. Beauchamp began as a sheep
station yonks ago but, like a lot of others, dwindled
away during the twentieth century. One night
between the wars the big old house got burnt to the
ground. The gardens got ploughed up. Pru and Guy
Blandwood bought the place when it was just a patch
of pine plantations and sheep paddocks. The first
thing they did was get some workmen to lay out new

grounds. Afterwards they got this house designed by Giles Morrin.

A dining room. A morning room. A music room.

'Guy had a law degree but it wasn't for him, the law,' murmurs Pru. 'And I had my degree in art history. We made up our minds to go on to the land. And this scrap of land came onto the market. West Canterbury is very much our stamping ground, and has been for our families since the year dot, so it all seemed to fall into place pretty nicely. We took it on and we've done our best to make our little bit of a mark.'

A library.

'Gorgeous,' I say, stopping at a double doorway to drool over its Palladian proportions – a perfect double cube. All four walls stacked with beautiful books. A twin set of french windows opening onto a courtyard. A twin set of leather sofas, oxblood red. A loo table, mahogany. Atop the loo table, an antique globe. The globe whirrs on its brass spindle when touched by me gingerly.

'Not very useful,' says my hostess. 'It's early Victorian.'

'The loo table?'

'The globe.'

Other rooms follow.

Gold. Silver. Silk. Tapestry.

'Gorgeous,' I say again. 'The whole house is gorgeous.'

'Well it's our home, and we hope it'll become the home of our grandchildren one day. Guy will show you the woodlands. Now, while we're waiting for him why don't we get out into the fresh air and take a little trot down the poplar avenue?'

So a little trot is what we take.

White flagstones between two towering rows of flaring yellow. One tall straight Lombardy after another tall straight Lombardy after another tall straight Lombardy. An easterly ruffles our hair and stirs the yellow leaves. Pru, clearly reckoning that she's done her bit, has gone quiet. Screwing up her pale grey eyes, she stares at a deer paddock. Is the ball now in my court? What can I say next?

Something pastoral.

'Good season, like?' I blather, not knowing the right words but supposing we must be at the start or the end or in the middle of some sort of season in her rural calendar. 'Like – so far?'

She gives me a short look, brisk and businesslike.

'Middling. Fairly good grass growth till a fortnight ago.'

'Weather behaving itself?'

I sound like my own granddad, poking about in his tiny backyard in the city.

'A few first frosts. Good enough ground moisture on the whole. Our stockman's happy.'

Her walking brogues, handmade, clearly bespoke, scuff through yellow drifts of leaf fall. Yellow leaves, golden paddocks. Above everything, the deep blue sky – deep blue, yet blank – of May. All of a sudden I feel aroused. I want it! The world of these people is like porn. You can easily get off on how fucking fabulous their lives are, how everything they've got is uber quality, how lucky they are, how privileged they are – how they've got everything, the lot!

'Awesome lookout, isn't it?' I say.

'Yes, it *is* rather pretty. We're quite lucky.'

A few of the deer lift soft skittish heads from the grass and look at us, some shying away. Poor things. Fenced in. Like me. Not like Pru.

I point to the haha that runs along both sides of the avenue.

'Digging this out must have been a lot of work! Why is it so deep and wide?'

'Well, the deer, you know. They're jumpers, Wayne.'

Not me. I'm no jumper. I'm a stumper.

'Did you start off with a vision for the whole garden, Pru?'

'Certainly. We wanted a Regency sort of look, but not forced, not like some gardens you see these days, where everything's been overdone. You know what I mean? Done too well.'

Sure, of course I know what she means, she means the gardens of upstarts who don't come from an old family and don't know there's any such thing as an old family but just blunder about thinking that all you need to do with some of the raw millions you made with hard mahi or more likely crooked trading is talk to pricey landscape architects and point at a pic or two inside a copy of some glossy mag – like my mag – and order a garden at x thousand smackers to the square metre.

'You both grew up in the country?'

'Yes, that's right.'

I know without asking. Again, our files back at the mag. Pru comes from an old landowning family. Her husband comes from an old landowning family. The two of them are cousins several times over, in fact, since the family trees in that toney old crowd are tangled together all the way up from root to canopy.

'Cool,' I say. 'Wide open spaces.'

'And narrow closed minds, I sometimes think,' she adds, which is startling but before I can follow up she's moved on. 'You yourself grew up in town, Wayne?'

'Dwayne,' I say, maybe too fast because she looks me up and down again, very politely but a bit sort of disdainfully.

'Sorry, Dwayne,' she says. 'Christchurch?'

'Yip, that's right. Avondale.'

'Avondale? I can't quite place Avondale. Anywhere near Avonhead?'

'Other side of town from Avonhead.'

The east side of town, needless to say. Pru can hardly be expected to be clear about those suburbs over there, to the east.

'Very nice,' she says with admirable calmness. 'And how long have you been with this magazine?'

'Couple months. Not my usual line of work.'

'Oh? What's your usual line?'

'Political journalism. I've been doing political news for a fair few years. I was the editor of a newspaper for expats in Mexico.'

'How interesting.'

Not interesting, in other words. I know that people like her think the only interesting places are here and Europe. I grew up seeing things a bit differently. I wanted to go everywhere, look at everything, so after getting my degree I backpacked through most of Asia. After that I came back, got married, saved. And then Annette – my wife – and me wandered around West Africa. A lot to learn in West Africa. Latin America was our next goal. We wound up in Oaxaca, in Mexico, where we ran out of money and had a go at getting work. Annette's a secondary teacher and found a job easily. I was by then a seasoned journo and found a job easily too. Annette stuck it out for a couple of years in Oaxaca. She got homesick, though. Off she flew. I stayed on. I love Mexico. Annette and me are divorced now. I loved Mexico more every year. Then the new tech started cutting into newspapers and I lost my job.

'You chose this sort of journalism for the sake of a change, I imagine?'

'I chose this sort of journalism for the sake of the pay.'

'I see.'

Her voice sounds serene but clearly she thinks my coarseness quite nasty. Anyone knows it's not on to speak so frankly about work, or lack of work, or money, or lack of money.

I could've stayed on in Oaxaca and looked for some other sort of work, maybe an online newssite, but it was time to get back here for a bit. Mum's on the way out. Her heart's dicky. Dad's already gone west. So I'm back in my boyhood bedroom in the same brick bungalow they brought us kids up in – three bedrooms, a lounge and a dinette – doing my best to keep an eye out for Mum, helping when I can

– she's not the sort who'll ask for help. My bro helps, too. And my sis.

I let out a bit of a sigh, thinking about poor old Mum.

Pru says nothing.

We get to a hexagonal pavement at the end of the avenue and stop, looking around us at the deer paddock. Centrepiece of the hexagon is an urn – a big urn – whose plinth and bowl are glazed cobalt and whose handles are a couple of terracotta cupids poking their little bare bums up at the sky.

'Italian, is it? The urn?'

'Good spotting. Yes, Tuscan. Not so terribly old, only the late eighteenth century. Its mate was broken so we were able to pick it up quite cheaply.'

Hah! Ceramics are big in Mexico. I've learnt enough interviewing plutocratic politicians and rich lobbyists over there not only to tell an Italian urn from a French urn but give a goodish guess as to the cost. You don't get your mitts on one of these things, even without its twin, unless you can shell out two or three months of my salary.

'Cool,' I say.

A taciturnity she seems to quite like.

'Shall we make our way back to the terrace, Dwayne? We can go down the yew avenue then, and find Guy.'

As we turn in our tracks, I see she's casting a cool measuring eye over everything. The creamy limestone walls of the terraces. The autumn colours of the trees. The creamy limestone walls of the nearest wing of the house. I feel cut off, left out. I feel that these people are guarding secrets they keep hidden from people like us, people like you and me. They know things we don't know, these people, don't they?

They pull the strings.

We set off down the yew avenue, which runs between the deer paddock on the left and a horse paddock on the right. A brown horse comes nosing over, dangling his long limp dick. He sticks his head across the fence, shakes a bit, snorts, and seems to offer himself to Pru.

Pru, letting out a little laugh, steps across to the fence and starts stroking the horse's snout. Is that what they call it? Or is it muzzle?

Or nuzzle?

Pru no longer looks cool and measuring. She looks happy. It's amazing how happy. So, if it was my tackle she was checking out – you know, earlier, when she seemed to look down at my pants – then my tackle hasn't passed muster. How come? I mean, I'm no male model but I'm not so fugly I need to sign up for plastic surgery. I work out at the gym, so I'm buff. Sort of. I know from covert surveillance operations in the changing rooms, too, that while there's nothing to be so very stoked about down there in the tackle shop, nor is there anything to be too shy about.

Pru would just rather look at a bloody horse than a sexy – well, ish – guy!

Weird, because why should a snorting bag of bones –

Why would a whiffy dobbin propped on top of four hooves and flicking a long hairy swatch behind its bum make someone so happy? A cat, I could get.

Or, at a push, a poodle. The ash blonde bob seems to quiver with happiness as my hostess shakes her own head from side to side, sort of matching her movements with the movements of the big hairy nag.

What does she see think she's seeing?

'Good boy,' she says over and over, getting her fingertips into his hair – or pelt, is it – or is it fur? 'Who's my boy? You, aren't you? You're my lovely boy.'

What is it she sees?

CHAPTER TWO

St Saviour's parish hall is hot and stuffy, if you have the good luck to get a seat in front of one of the electric radiators. If you don't, it's freezing. A chilly white oblong, that's the hall. White walls, white ceiling, floor covered by a robust industrial carpet, charcoal grey, crisscrossed with lines of pale grey. A sampler of Maori needlework, red and black, on each of the two window walls. One sampler shows those spirally things. What are they called? Koru! The other shows rows of triangles. So we're up with the times, though nobody in our congregation is Maori.

We approve the minutes of the last meeting and go on to the treasurer's statement. Jayden is our vestry treasurer because, being owner of a coffee shop, he's the only one of us who knows how to balance books.

'I move that we accept the treasurer's statement,' I say.

'Cheers, Pru,' grunts Jim. 'Seconder?'

'Second,' says Buffy.

'Ayes?' barks Jim. 'Carried!'

Jim likes getting through things briskly. She bulks large at the head of the table and her hair has been shoved back with a no-nonsense Alice band. A murky band of brown and off-white looking a bit like a rasher of bacon left too long before frying. Jim often wears Alice bands.

'Can't *bear* anything getting in my way,' she always says. 'I like to see a *good* clear bit of country ahead!'

The vicar sits quietly. A vicar generally chairs vestry meetings, of course, but not our vicar and not our vestry. Phattaraporn, the vicar's companion, will bring in supper after an hour or so. Almost all of us are holding out for that tea and those scones. Our vicar likes peace and she likes quiet. Jim, on the other hand – well, let's just say dear old Jim doesn't mind awfully if things begin with peace and quiet but then bolt the other way. Almost the only thing she has in common with the vicar is that they both look forward to the supper. Phattaraporn has become a dab hand at baking scones, which is not bad for someone who grew up in Bangkok.

We work our way through the agenda. The clock ticks. A need for a new parish electoral roll. The clock keeps ticking. A question about a leaky tap in the cemetery. Not long now till supper.

'*Next* and *last* order of business, fundraising for the tower,' says Jim. '*What* are we going to auction?'

The tower is in a pretty bad way. Our church is stone, blocks of basalt. Thousands and thousands will need to be shovelled into the kitty to get the tower back up to the mark. We managed to raise only a paltry fifteen hundred from the spring fete last year, and nothing since, so we really need to give things a good nudge along. We made up our minds at the last vestry meeting to hold a midwinter dinner and auction to try to bring in a decent sum towards the work.

'Handicrafts, perhaps?' I say.

'No, Pru,' says Buffy. 'We need big ticket items.'

'Big *ticket* items?' snorts Jim. 'You sound like a *shop*keeper, Buffy!'

Buffy, while one of us in every way – in other words anything but a shopkeeper – tends to get on Jim's goat. Today her hair is honey blonde. Her lipstick is a touch too pink. She looks around the table, inviting us into a conspiracy. I look straight back.

I do so dislike people ganging up on other people.

'Jim, you know perfectly well what I mean. We can't just be jogging along with dribs and drabs. We've got to get people really digging into their pockets.'

'Hmf,' says Jim.

'Buffy's right,' chips in Flea.

'Yes,' says Midge.

'Sweet,' says Jayden, whose sibilants seem to go on forever, 'but what sort of big ticket item?'

'Why not art?' says Buffy.

'Art?' says Jim. '*Art*?'

Jim and I are first cousins through her father and my mother, or in other words she's a Carrel. Imogene Carrel of Trecarrel. She was nicknamed Jimjim when she was little. Hard to think of her ever being little! Afterwards, of course, it got shortened to Jim. Although she's a good thirteen years senior to me, her fame as an old girl lived on during my school days at St Margaret's. The cause of that fame was her prowess with a hockey stick. Jim was captain of the first eleven, at least till she went for the shins of the captain of St Hilda's. She scored a double hit. Our headmistress, while doing her best to seem scandalised, secretly admired Jim's spirit.

'Your cousin Imogen – loyal!' the headmistress once said to me over a sherry or two.

Jim is the only one of the family left living on Trecarrel. Uncle Gilbert years ago inherited the place but killed himself with a shotgun. Word was – it was all a bit of a scandal – that he was in love with a young shearer but his feelings weren't requited by the boy. Uncle Alfred took over the place after Gilbert. He died ten years ago and a family trust runs Trecarrel. Jim and her sisters share the earnings. Cordelia lives with a husband and has a nice stud stable on a sheep station in Marlborough. Ophelia lives in Tuscany. Jim rattles around our district in a battered old Land Rover, hairy and smelly with dogs. I mean both are hairy and smelly. The Land Rover, and poor old Jim! Watery green eyes stare out at you from a wide ruddy face harrowed by half a century of riding in all weathers, stalking for deer in the back country, mustering sheep, heaving cast ewes out of ditches. And when she talks she does tend to roar, as though fighting a norwester while climbing the scree face of Mount Hare.

'I'd be willing to donate a watercolour,' says Buffy. 'Still life – flowers – inherited it from an aunt.'

'I've got an etching or two I don't like,' says Flea.

'We could ask the landscape painting group if they'd be willing to cough up one of those daubs they're always cranking out,' says Midge. 'Alpine spurs or snowbound gorge, sort of style.'

Flea and Midge have always been thick as thieves. Felicity and Margery. Flidge is my nickname for the two of them. The three of us were at St Margaret's during my day. Buffy was there too. Head girl in our last year. Flea and Midge, two years younger, had a desperate crush on Buffy.

'An ex of mine is a painter who does male nudes,' says Jayden. 'He might pony up with one, if I schmooze him right.'

Buffy, Flea and Midge roll their eyes at one another, unseen by Jayden. All three of them think he's – well, we know nothing about his family. He hasn't got a family, in the sense that we mean family. He grew up somewhere in Christchurch. He takes pains to avoid saying where, exactly. After opening his coffee shop in the township he began turning up at church, bowing to the altar as though it were high church, which it isn't – none of that silliness – and getting himself voted onto the vestry. Not that he had to elbow out of the way any competitors for such a thankless task. And ever since then he's been doing his level best to try to fit in with our crowd, the poor lamb.

'What a fun idea, Jayden,' I chip in. 'Guy and I have got simply stacks of dreary old oils just gathering dust.'

Jim starts to sway.

'*We-e*-ell,' she says, weighing the word slowly to keep Buffy and her clique on tenterhooks. 'If we're going to go down *that* particular track I've got some very nice horse brasses we could try to flog off.

And, while I've got the bit between my teeth, I wonder if old Jock might let us have some of his interwar *saddlery*.'

Silence.

A look swapped between Flea, Midge and Buffy.

Jim has the odd blind spot, of course, as we all do. Well, in her case quite a few blind spots. One of which is horses. Jim's very fond of horses. Jim loves horses. Buffy, one of the people I think of as a long blinker, breaks her record for long-blinking while the vicar, sensing trouble afoot, hunkers down inside the turtleneck of her baggy bottle-green jumper.

'Now, Jim,' begins Buffy in a kindly way warning everyone to tuck their own chins down into their own metaphorical turtlenecks, 'far be it from me to dampen your enthusiasm, but I do think – now I don't know how to say this quite as tactfully as I might wish, and I certainly have no intention of causing offence, but – I really do feel that we need to keep the auction strictly horse-free, as opposed to the debacle of the spring fete which was, may I say, over-horsed?'

The hair rises on nearly every head.

'*What* do you mean!' trumpets Jim. '*Over-*horsed!'

'Over-horsed,' repeats Buffy, failing to quail.

'Well, I think we can all agree that the *ploughing* exhibition was not, on the whole, a success,' says Jim. 'I'll admit that the mud was pretty dire. And I can only apologise *again*, Buffy, for the way my Meg happened to be standing alongside you when she dropped her dung. But then, as you *may* recall, I did rather think that scarlet leather wasn't *quite* the thing for a spring fete, and Clydesdales may look stolid, but like any horse they'll jib or jink at anything they fancy *uncanny*. I do advise khaki, grey or *navy* for the next fete.'

Buffy darts a quick look sideways. Flea and Midge nod and smile on cue. The vicar dives even deeper into her turtleneck. Jayden, wanting to please everyone, looks up at the ceiling. Harry Hall, our other vestryman, sits bolt upright, awakened from a quiet snooze by the sixth sense of a seasoned hunter telling him a war trumpet is now braying and there's a likelihood of blood.

'Jim, I don't think you quite understand,' says Buffy very quietly and very slowly. 'We really mustn't have any of your horsey nonsense.'

Harry's bloodshot eyes are glinting now. That war trumpet braying. Jayden crosses and uncrosses his legs. The vicar eyes up the doorway.

Jim opens her mouth, then shuts it.

Nobody speaks.

Jim opens her mouth.

I think of a salmon some adroit angler has landed onto a clump of tussock alongside a lake in the High Country. Nobody, at least to my knowledge, has been quite this blunt with Jim since last spring when a saleswoman at Quinn's in Merivale told her the shop did not, and never would, stock a size twenty-two moleskin pant.

'*Non*sense!' she blusters. '*Every*body enjoys horses!'

'I think you'll recall the exhibition of ploughing with Clydesdales made no money and quite a few people were upset by the damage done to their shoes from having to wade through all that mud and muck, and not only those among us who were wearing scarlet leather,' goes on Buffy. 'I'm right about the money, aren't I, Jayden?'

Jayden, on the spot now, notices that the ceiling needs to be inspected still more closely.

'*Jay*den?' gruffly says Jim.

He flinches.

'Well, er, yes, to be perfectly frank with you, er Jim, we lost on the ploughing. By the time we'd paid off the dry cleaning bills and little Sophie's orthodontist's bill – '

'Silly kid, didn't her parents *tell* her that horses kick! I still don't see why we should have forked out.'

'Well, very true,' stumbles on Jayden, 'but we did agree here at the vestry, if you remember, to cover that cost, and only two votes against – '

Jim and Harry were the two votes. Harry believes in not sparing the rod. He got thrashed daily to within an inch of his life when a boy at Christ's College, if you believe his stories, and if you keep believing his stories it never did him anything but good. I voted to pay for the orthodontist. I seldom vote against Jim but thought it was pretty hard on people who had turned up for what they'd supposed would be a stroll across dry turf and instead found themselves wallowing in a swamp watching Clydesdales pass wind, and pass other things too.

'I *am* the chair, for heaven's sake,' growls Jim, 'and *do* have quite a weight of executive work on my shoulders – '

She looks accusingly at the vicar, who now also notices that the ceiling needs to be inspected closely.

Time for me to make a move and do what I do so often, soothe the group.

'Interesting ideas, everyone!' I cheep. 'An art auction does seem to be the way to go, and we've got some very useful ideas to be working on, haven't we? Perhaps we're now entitled to reward ourselves with a cup of tea?'

Jim, huffing, stands up and stalks towards the doorway.

'Don't *want* bloody tea!'

Off she stumps. I know not to follow. Always best to leave her be, in this sort of crisis. Tact has never been her strong suit, dear old Jim. I've often had to glide in her wake with a vial of oil to calm the troubled waters she churns up. I'll phone her when I get out to the car. As for Buffy – well, her behaviour was quite uncalled for, of course. No doubt she'll understand that when she gets home and has a snifter and, although it would be asking too much to anticipate anything like an apology, I imagine she'll pull her horns in a bit at the next vestry meeting.

I wonder, on occasion, whether giving my time to the vestry is worthwhile. I can't understand why people get so jumpy. A vestry's only a vestry, for goodness sake. We're not drawing up the Treaty of Versailles.

At times like this – looking on, listening in, trying my best to tone down the worst of the miniature manoeuvres, the tiny trouncings, tinny triumphs, of

this or that troublemaker on that or this committee –
well, I just long to go away, right away. I clench my
jaw – secretly. I struggle to stop myself from
yawning – secretly.

I feel so sleepy. I feel so heavy.

I find myself asking –

Is this it?

I mean to say – you know. This! All this – this
silly stuff. Parish pump. The garden, the house,
dinners, drinks. Always everything so utterly
ordinary. Not one single thing out of the ordinary has
happened to me for simply – well, for years. Has
anything out of the ordinary ever happened to me,
really? I suppose now and then something pops up.
Today, for example, it was a bit of fun doing the
honours for that chap, that journalist chap. What was
his name? Darren? Oh dear, I did muff that once or
twice, didn't I? I hope I didn't hurt his feelings. He
seemed nice enough, though quite clearly he didn't
know a fencepost from a cattle stop.

Anyway, going back to what I was saying –

My life, and so forth – is this it?

We don't really live, do we? Well, to be frank
with myself, for once – you know – why can't I be
frank, at least with myself, even if I'm not frank with
anyone else? I mean – why the hell do I live my life
this way? Only a few weeks till I turn fifty, and what
have I – what have I done or felt or – or – ?

I mean – really!

Only –

Now look here, Pru, buck yourself up, for
goodness sake. You know perfectly well you've got
a perfectly good life, so stop your bleating. You

know you're awfully lucky. You've got Guy. You've got the offs. Well, we've both got the offs. The offspring, that's our nickname for Tim and Charley. Admittedly it'd be nicer if they weren't so far away. Charley in London. Tim in Hong Kong. Anyway, the offs, Guy, heaps of friends and family. Money, it goes without saying. I know it's not to be sneezed at, having a bit of money. And health, and a hobby or two, and –

Yes, a lovely life!

Phattaraporn pads in with the tea trolley.

'I see Charley's in the latest *Tatler*, looking lovely,' says Midge leaning towards me as we take a first sip.

'Oh?'

I don't altogether trust Midge.

'Mm. A charity do. She was with a royal. What was the caption? Oh yes. Charlotte Blandwood, being charitable. I see she's blonde now, more or less the same shade as Buffy.'

'Is she? Well she's been blonde once or twice.'

'Has she lost even more weight? I think it's criminal the way models are made to starve themselves these days.'

'She was never a big eater.'

Charley calls, oddly enough, as soon as I get to the car and turn on my phone, ready to ring Jim.

'Mummy!'

'Hi darling. All well at your end?'

'Oh totally, totally, darling – feeling a bit run down, mind you – burning the candle at both ends!

Hugh and Helen had a gang of us over at their place last night – it was a bit of a trek getting out to Gloucestershire – and between you and me, not so very sure it was worth the rubber – she's not much fun, these days – you know, what with being pregnant. Well, frankly, she's become bloody boring, haha – so a group of us tooled back to town to do the clubs.'

'Hugh and Helen?'

'You know, Hugh and Helen Netherly. She's one of my best mates – Lady Helen, daughter of that boozy old bastard Lord Styx. Hugh's her husband – nice enough – he's next in line for the earldom of Netherly.'

We chat for ten minutes or so about parties, clothes, parties, people, clothes, parties. Actually it's mostly Charley chatting and me listening, or rather me letting most of her words go in one ear and out the other. I don't feel the need to listen too closely. She's never needed babying.

'Best get my skates on, darling,' she winds up. 'Got to get out to Heathrow.'

'Off somewhere gorgeous?'

'Totally! Amalfi coast – a few of us heading away for a few days – bound to be a lot of fun! I'm starving, better grab some breakfast – I might just finish off a bottle of Bolly someone's left lying around in the flat. Not a lot of carbs in that, haha!'

CHAPTER THREE

A new morning. A new day. I bumble downstairs in my silk mules and my merino dressing gown to find Guy where I know I'll always find him at this hour of the morning, seated at the kauri kitchen table making notes in the garden log. He hunches awkwardly when working on the log. He doesn't know he hunches and I don't know how to tell him about it, poor boy. He's got on a pair of grey moleskin trousers and a baggy old Fairisle jersey. Guy always wears moleskins and a jersey when knocking about home at this time of year. A jacket of Harris tweed, grey flecked with green and burgundy, has been thrown over the back of a chair. He'll have worn the jacket while doing his round of the grounds.

I know all his ways, and he knows all my ways.

'Sleep well, darling?' he says before smearing toast with rhubarb jam and taking a bite.

'As ever, sweetheart,' I reply. 'Ten hours, nearly.'

We've wondered sometimes whether the way I sleep so long and so heavily is quite healthy. Guy, by contrast, sleeps exactly seven hours every night, no more and no less. On my way to the toaster, shuffling in my mules, I glance down at the garden log.

Malus s03, blight on two lower leaves.

Malus s03 stands for the third malus sylvestris in the row on the right side of the sundial. Malus sylvestris is wild crabapple. I never write up the garden log. Guy's the one with the neat handwriting.

Chrysanthemum ns20-39, last buds opening.
The second bed of Nantyderry sunshine chrysanthemums, lovely things. They grow in a sheltered sunny aspect along one of the terrace walls.

The garden log is one of my poor old boy's hobby horses. Botany in general is one of his hobby horses. He likes to find out not only the right botanical name but every single vernacular name of everything that grows. One can point him at a bit of greenery and he'll do his damnedest to classify it according to order, family, genus, species. Anything from a modest moss to a towering totara. Nor is it only botany. He likes every sort of taxonomy. I think he thinks that classification makes things understandable, and I dare say he's right.

As for me – well, in my head I sometimes seem to go in for quite a lot of boundary blurring.

Only in my head, mind you.

I slot slices of wholemeal bread into the toaster and take a first taste of coffee. We don't ask Tanya to make the breakfast. She needs to get her little ones ready for the school bus and sort her own place out before she can start working on ours. Anyway, it doesn't seem right to ask someone to toast a few slices of bread and make a pot of coffee, does it?

More's the pity.

'What's on the agenda today, darling?' asks Guy, turning a page of the log.

'One or two turns on the treadmill, sweetheart. A quick call on Buffy. Vestry stuff. At some point I'll look in on Mummy. Afterwards, a word to swap with the vicar and a few things to pick up at St Saviour's.

Guerrilla war is still being fought between Jim and the anti-Jims.'

'No rest for the wicked,' murmurs Guy.

'The usual for you, Guysie?'

'The usual, Pwu.'

The rendezvous over the coffee pot and toaster is when we first catch sight of one another, since we sleep in separate rooms, each with its own bathroom – though in the same wing of the house, of course, the east wing. We like the chance to be together, just the two of us, over the table at breakfast.

'That chap from that magazine,' I mention as we push back our chairs, get up and gather together the cutlery and crockery, 'sent an email to say a photographer will be coming later today if the sky is a bit overcast.'

'Overcast? I wonder why?'

'Oh it's to do with light. A clear bright sky is no good, unless you catch it very early or very late in the day.'

'Why ever not? I would've thought it optimal.'

'Something to do with length of the sun's rays. I learnt that when doing the photography paper in my degree. The rays of the sun bleach the image.'

'A bright light kills the illusion of life, then?'

'Every cloud has a silver lining.'

'Hah!'

After breakfast his next step will be to saddle up his hack and do the rounds of the woodlands and paddocks. He's not what you might call a joiner, not like me. I envy him, sometimes, the way he shrugs off joining. Yet if none of us was a joiner, where would we all be?

Disjointed?

I scuff back upstairs. I shower myself. I towel myself dry. I dress myself. I step through to the landing. An oval of old glass, very faintly greenish and slightly warped with age, shows me peering at myself in a lacklustre way. I'm too short, too stocky. My face is too round. My eyes are a very uninteresting grey. My hair is more or less all right. My clothes will do. A suit of pale cream linen with pearl buttons. A string of pearls – my ordinary single string of pearls – around my neck. Also, spearing the lobes on either side of my head, my ordinary pearl earrings. No point dressing up. I'm only popping in to the township.

Who's going to be looking?

Nobody, really.

The oval of old glass is framed in mahogany, carved with leaves of laurel, topped by a cartouche showing the crest of the Tancreds. The piece has been handed down through my family. A lot of things in the house come from my family. A lot of other things come from the Blandwoods.

Taupe court shoes on my feet. My handbag is taupe, too.

'Morning, Tanya!' I sing out while making my way through the house on track to the garage. 'I'm off to the township.'

'No worries, Pru!' she sings back.

We're so lucky to have Tanya. We've always been lucky with staff. Well, give or take the odd horror story. Our grooms, every man jack of them, have been good. Our gardeners too. Our nanny, who worked wonders when the offs were tots, was first rate. I was even blessed for many years with the best cleaning woman one could wish for, the sort of person who went out of her way to track down every unwelcome smear, each unwanted spot.

I keep on trotting towards the garage.

I'll take the Mercedes.

I wish it was one of the days I go for a spin up to town, which I do every few weeks for the sake of an outing – shopping, since it can be fun to have a bit of a dig around in the shops, and getting together with old friends for drinks or dinner and perhaps afterwards putting up for a night at The George. I don't have a lot of time for shopping. I'm always too busy, or pretty nearly.

I roll down the driveway, turn right onto the road to Hare Forest.

Paddocks stretch out, dead flat, on all sides. Plantations strut in point-blank rows. Straight roads fly off at sharp angles, a few making for a township, a few seeking out narrow points between streams, a few taking off towards a bridge and one striking out for where, long ago, there was a ferry. The roads make you think that in colonial days a squad of archers took a stand at varying points all over the plains and then shot arrows off towards the points of the compass, after which roads were surveyed along the pathways of the arrows.

Oh dear, I simply don't want to pay that quick call on Buffy.

Buffy and Flea and Midge, and – and so many of the people who sit on committees – really, I think – well, the vestry is pretty time consuming, even though the meetings are only monthly. Always there seems to be so much running around, and it's not as though it's my only – you know, I've got the West Canterbury Agricultural and Pastoral Association and I get run ragged by my work with the committee of the Worthington Youth Cancer Foundation.

The paddocks are getting too dry.

I go through a crossroads, swing around a shallow bend, and here's Hare Forest. Cottages in a row. A few bungalows. The old county offices, white and neoclassical , now Jayden's coffee shop, Espress Yourself. The wrought iron gates to the domain. One or two shops. The cenotaph, white stone. The war memorial hall, pink stucco and squat.

A few more bungalows.

Folk on the road give me a wave or a smile as I go by, because of course I know everyone and everyone knows me. I'm a Tancred, after all. Tancred of Saxon Downs. Saxon Downs is being run these days by my brother, Guy. Yes, he's Guy too. A bit bewildering, isn't it? We do tend to stick to our old family names.

Flowers are fading in the gardens of the township cottages and bungalows. I adore the changing seasons. Or rather – well, I adore spring, but autumn – it makes you think of dying, doesn't it? Silly to think that way. Or, at least, to think that there's something wrong in thinking about dying. You can't have life without death, can you? Nor can you have death without life. We all know that, all of us who live on the land. Autumn lets you look back calmly. You look forward, too. The first fall of snow. The opening of the ski season on Mount Hare. After that, our two months of holiday in Spain and Italy. And then, back home for the tail end of the ski season, and then, well –

And then the spring blossoms!

There's always something to be getting on with in life, and it doesn't pay to be too intense about anything.

I'll pop in on Mummy before seeing Buffy.

Mummy's slowing down these days. Goes without saying, really, given she's within hailing distance of eighty. Yet she always turns herself out perfectly. A hardworking woman, too, during her heyday. She did an awful lot when I was young. It's a very full life for a woman on a sheep station. She had so much to manage, but she saw to it. She had three kids, for a start, and of course had to keep us on our toes while managing everything when Daddy was away with all his many doings. She knew the station nearly as well as he did. Also, she had a position in the county. You know. Chairwoman of this, chairwoman of that. A lot of charitable work. She wasn't showy about it. Quite the opposite of showy.

Here we are, the entrance to Saxon Downs. The brick gateposts, topped with cannon balls.

The avenue of silver poplars.

A light warm norwester has sprung up. The poplar leaves flick over, in waves, showing silver undersides. Other leaves flick over, in another wave, showing olivine oversides. The flicking is like a sort of semaphore, or so I used to think when I was a girl. The flicking seems like a kind of morse code. On, off, off, on, off –

What are the leaves saying?

Live, die, die, live –

I suppose a girl these days wouldn't think of morse, she'd think of digital coding. A computer programme. Yet no matter what type of code, I still don't know what the leaves are saying.

Off, on, on –

Die, live –

Daddy won't be at Saxon Downs. He's away shooting deer in the high country. Shooting at his age! Always comes up trumps, does Daddy. Admittedly he can be, well – gruff, I suppose you might say. At times, you know, when I was a tot, he seemed quite frightening. His standards were exacting and are still exacting. Daddy's absolutely a gentleman, too, someone who can be counted on to do and say everything right. And he's carrying on the same way up to the present day. That's simply how he is. A wonderful man, but not always an easy man. So in one sense it's a teeny bit of a relief he's away shooting.

I swing towards the turning circle in front of the portico. The house, red brick, looms up on its wide sweep of green turf. Virginia creeper, crawling over the gables of the upper storey, burns bright red under the low sunrays.

A fantail darts across the driveway.

Actually, between you and me, he's never thought much of Guy. Daddy, I mean, has never thought much of Guy. My husband Guy, not my brother Guy. Daddy behaves well towards him, of course, but doesn't really approve of the way he seems to be sort of frittering away his life, you know, not doing anything very useful in the world, not joining committees, just keeping his nose in his books.

Guy, on his side, has always been a tiny bit frightened of Daddy.

A pity. Yet there you go.

The heels of my court shoes are crunching on the gravel as I walk towards the portico.

'Mummy!' I sing out. 'Cooeee!'

Her hearing isn't the best these days. The poor dear will be in the morning room, I dare say. My home life was wonderful but it was fun to get away to prep school after my ninth birthday. Cried a bit, but that's par for the course. A group of girls and I became fast friends, the way you do at boarding school. Afterwards, we stuck together at St Margaret's. At varsity we stuck together, too. My schoolfriends, with their brothers and cousins. Dances, tennis. The odd drink or two. Or three. I didn't take up drugs. Anyway, jolly japes at varsity, but I wasn't really sure what to do when I graduated in art history. Mummy stepped in to the breach and bought me a little gallery in Christchurch. She used her own money, nothing from Daddy. The gallery was in a good spot, just off Oxford Terrace.

The job of running it, mind you, proved not too fascinating. And the bookkeeping – I found it pretty baffling.

Guy and I, meanwhile, had begun going about together – though of course we already knew each other inside out. Cousins, moving among the same circles here in West Canterbury. He'd got his law degree and gone into the family firm, Tancred Tancred Carrel Blandwood. Younger sons in his family always go into Tancred Tancred Carrel Blandwood.

'Honestly,' he said to me one afternoon as we were watching polo, 'it's dreary.'

'What's dreary? Polo?'

'The law.'

'Oh.'

'Memory, mostly.'

'The law, you mean, when you say mostly memory?'

'Yes, the bloody boring law. It's all about precedent, the law.'

West Canterbury at that point stuck up their mallets, appealing for a foul. West were playing Marlborough. I don't care a lot for polo. Nor does Guy. Yet we'd tagged along because we thought it the right thing to do, to fly the flag. The green of the turf was pretty enough, together with the darkness of the evergreens behind the field. And the team colours. West Canterbury wear azure and white.

'I'd walk away from the law tomorrow, if I knew what I really wanted to do, Pru.'

Only he didn't say my name quite right. The poor boy suffers from a teeny bit of a lisp, so what he really said was *I'd walk away from the law tomowwow, if I knew what I weally wanted to do, Pwu.* The lisp is sweet.

I leaned towards him sort of confidingly.

'Pwu,' I whispered, wanting to say it the way he says it, yet not wanting to hurt his feelings.

'What – ?'

He drew his head back, looking as though he'd been slapped. He squinted down at me, blushing. I felt awful. Yet somehow I still wanted to keep saying my name the way he said it, because it was so endearing.

'Sorry, terribly sorry, but – but – I just love it, the way you say it.'

'Love it?'

He was wholly out of his depth, I could see clearly.

A new chukker was beginning. West Canterbury was doing well enough, but so was Marlborough. The men pounded back and forth, mallets flying. The ball whistled when whacked – polo balls were still wooden in those days – while clods of turf were being kicked up by the hooves of this or that pony.

'Love – you, Guy. I love you.'

'What!'

As though nobody could love him, as though he wasn't loveable.

A great-aunt of mine, who had lots of money, died the following week. I got some of the money. Guy got some of the money, too, since she was also his great-aunt. We got quite a bit, really. He made up his mind to call it quits with the law and I made up my mind to call it quits with the gallery. We got married and bought Beauchamp. All went smoothly. After a year or two the offs came along. And now they're grown up!

And here I am, back at Saxon Downs.

My heels are clacking onto the veranda. I'll give an hour or so to Mummy. She'll be wanting to interrogate me about the plans for my fiftieth birthday party. Our fiftieth birthday party, actually. Mine and Guy's. We were born, oddly enough, in the same year and on the same day. Winter babies, that's us. We're going to give a big dinner. All our nearest and dearest. Well, not the offs. Not worth winging their way across whole oceans simply for the sake of a slice of birthday cake!

'Mummy, darling – you're looking gorgeous, as always,' I say, a bit forced, a bit over-hearty.

A hearty note because it's clear she's been looking out at the world, from her sofa in the morning room, a trifle stonily.

'Hmph,' she says, turning and looking me up and down. 'And you look – nice.'

'Don't be too lavish with the compliments, darling,' I say, with a bit of a nervous laugh.

'Well perhaps you could drop a pound or two, though you always were more terrier than greyhound.'

Poor darling, not in the best of tempers this morning. Awful, isn't it, growing old?

A few hours later – Mummy ticked off my list, followed by Buffy – I'm back in the township, sitting inside the coffee shop. I don't want a coffee really. I'm here because it's good to spend the odd dollar or two in the township. Jayden has hung hunting prints all over Espress Yourself. You know the style. Red cheeked folk in red jackets looking jolly.

Oh dear.

I hear the shop door open with a little ping.

A man comes through the door. A man my age, in a suit. Not a bad suit. A man with some taste and a bit of money, or credit. A businessman or lawyer or land agent. Someone passing through the township. Jayden bustles, speaking to the man just that little bit too fulsomely. The man, having given his order, seats himself, eases back, takes a cool survey of the other inmates of the shop.

Three of the local schoolteachers. Two tourists. Me.

He smiles at me.

Oh.

That sort of smile. You know. Well, a nice little boost for the ego. Above all after visiting Mummy! Yet – well, why would I? I mean, look at him! I want to yawn at the sight of him. Men like him, they get cranked out by the dozen in Cashmere and Merivale. I can imagine everything that man might do, say, think.

What would be the point?

Guy and I have shut up shop in the way of passion. Well, we never were so very passionate. Neither of us is that type. We did want kids, of course. The offs. I made willing, though when it comes to bed and that sort of thing, to be honest I really don't know what all the fuss is about and a few years of marriage certainly do strip away the mystery. We gave up sleeping together some years ago. Our sex life simply stopped in its tracks.

I don't mind. I pretty much never seem to think about sex, really.

We've got a good marriage. We rub along together very well. Guy always pops his head into my room to say goodnight. He's my very, very best friend. Opposites attracting, in a way. I mean, while we're both from the same background, and so forth, when it comes to personality we're not at all alike. Not really. Guy is quite shy. Well, I've said that already, haven't I?

'A quiet life is a good life, Pwu,' he says.

Not that I always let him live quietly! Occasionally, every fortnight or so, I'll take the crop to him and get him into his best bib and tucker and he'll squire me out to this or that party. He jibs, but I have my way.

A lot of jibbing went on before he was brought around to what I wanted for our birthday party.

'I think we'll seat thirty,' I said one night when we began the planning. 'We'll start by drawing up a short list.'

'A lot of to-do, don't you think, simply to feed and water the same people we've been seeing all our lives?' he said, seated by my side and speaking the teeniest bit querulously. 'None of us will say anything worth saying.'

'Guysie, you're too clever not to know perfectly well that a party's not about what you say, or at least not the literal meaning of what you say.'

He held up his hands in mock horror.

'All right, I surrender!'

'Good boy.'

He can be counted on to be a good boy. I've never heard an angry word, never glimpsed an angry look, from Guy.

A cake swallowed, my coffee sipped – the former too sweet, the latter bitter – I get up, step outside and stroll towards the Mercedes. Oops! Jean has heaved into view. A very old woman, she was once our cook at Saxon Downs. Quite a sight these days. A baggy acrylic jersey, polyester slacks and polymer boots she's forgotten to lace up. The trick is to keep her happy without letting her pin back your ears for too long spinning yarns – yarns spun I don't know how many times before – about the good old days at Saxon Downs.

'What about that day your mum and dad left you behind at the gymkhana? You remember? How they drove all the way home before they saw they'd forgotten you? Your mum laughed and laughed about that. And then when they sent the roustabout to find you, you was sobbing your wee head off.'

'Yes, I remember. How old was I again?'

'Couldn't of been more than seven, I reckon,' she says, spattering me – when she gets to the seven – with a somewhat unfortunate gob of spit. 'Those were the days!'

'Yes, Jean,' I say smilingly. 'Those were indeed the days.'

'And you remember how after that you was always worried? You was always worried they wouldn't bring you back. You know, whenever you went away? A real little worrier, that was you too right.'

'I do remember, Jean. I was quite the silly billy.'

I'm pretty adroit at dealing with all our old hands, if I do say so myself, and soon get myself away.

A spin down the road and before too long I'm back at Beauchamp. I pull into our garage, park the car and pop out a side door for a quiet wander through the topiary. Guy's very keen on the topiary. He takes a lot of pains to make sure our gardener keeps each and every shrub clipped into a nice tight cone or sphere or cube. As for me, well at this time of the day I adore the soft fragrances of the korokia and pittosporum and myrtles and – and right now, rounding the flank of a big holly cut like a corkscrew, I clap eyes on a thin man seated on a green garden bench in front of a row of box balls.

A man who's not only thin but somehow – meagre – somehow nothing.

A man hard even to describe, really. A haze of grey around his gawky long legs. A smudge of greyish green tweed around his narrow weedy trunk. Brown brogues. Pepper-and-salt hair, thinning. Eyes of pallid blue –

I blink.

The man becomes, once more, dear old Guy.

Guy, gripping a white porcelain cup of red tea, looking a trifle out of sorts. The eyes of pallid blue are watery. His nose is moist. Creeping down one of his narrow cheeks is a little slug of snot.

I sit down on the bench and see a letter tucked under his bottom.

'You look as though you've been in the wars, sweetheart. Something wrong?'

He lets out a sigh, slowly.

'Bertie,' he says.

'Bertie?'

'A letter in the post. A lawyer's letter. I've got the letter here with me – somewhere – well I had it a moment ago. A letter from Apia.'

'You're sitting on it, silly. Apia? In Italy?'

'Samoa, darling. Bertie's dead. You never knew him and now you never will know him. He was a good man.'

'Bertie? Bertie who went troppo?'

Amazingly, the answer is a sob.

Not once in my life, until today, have I heard Guy let out a sob. Yet it's only Bertie Blandwood. Bertie, his father's youngest brother. Bertie, my second cousin once removed, as well as my third cousin once removed, and – well, you know the drill. Bertie! Opening my arms to offer a hug – a bit ungainly, given that we're both seated side-by-side – I cast my mind back over everything I've ever known – well, not known, really – all I ever heard was gossip, and all I ever saw was a glimpse of an occasional family photo – anyway, everything filed away in my memory under the heading *Bertram Blandwood*. A tall thin man who looked to be the typical Blandwood yet who was talked about quite a lot, for a year or two, long ago. A man who was a bit of an oddball. An oddball who went awry. Or that's what people say.

A puzzle, really.

Why has my poor boy been crying?

Bertram Blandwood, how was he an oddball? How did he go awry? I don't know. Where did he go? Well, that I do know. He wandered about the world. He disembarked in likely spots. London, Venice, Istanbul. Afterwards he disembarked in less likely spots. Narvik, Veracruz, Valparaiso. One day he fetched up in Samoa, and that was where he chose to stay. He came home once, for a short and famously awful visit, when Guy was a little boy. He behaved outrageously, people say, by wearing a sarong sort of thing to a dinner party at Whiterock. Also he'd been smoking weed. He jeered at polo and polocrosse. He sneered at cricket and the West Canterbury Hunt. He made belittling remarks about the National Party.

Well, that's what people say. He made mock of everybody.

'He was a good man,' again says Guy.

'Was he, Guysie?'

'He was very good to me, Pwu. He went out of his way to walk with me, and to talk. He talked about the birds. He talked about the trees. He read me books. *The Wind in the Willows. Moominsummer Madness.* He gave me a tortoiseshell comb. He gave me – well, he gave me kindness.'

My phone begins bleeping.

'Tim,' I say.

'Wonders never cease,' says Guy.

Our son couldn't in any fairness be accused of being tied to our apron strings. He seldom phones more than once a month, if that. But then boys are boys, aren't they? We wouldn't want them to be clingy.

'Tim, lovely to hear from you, darling!' I chirp into the phone. 'All well?'

'All cool, Ma,' he drawls back. 'You and Pops?'

'Fit and well, sweetheart. We're together in the topiary right now, a lovely autumn day. Clear and dry. How's the weather in Hong Kong?'

'Weather means nothing in Hong Kong. We're inside glass cells all day, Ma. I just called Pops but his phone's off. Maybe put yours on loudspeaker so he can hear too? Something to say to the two of you. An update about doings at Kwok and Kwok.'

Tim is a merchant banker and sits at a teak desk on the sixtieth storey of the Hong Kong Asia Finance Centre. He handles most of our money. I mean by our money the investment capital handed down to us by our families over the years. The earnings from those funds pay our living costs. Beauchamp loses money, given that we don't run it as a working property. Kwok and Kwok is a company he's underwritten for us. A company to do with finance. A mortgage company, I think, with lots of its money in housing, or something, in the United States.

'Right you are, Tim,' I say, switching the phone to loudspeaker.

'Cheers, Ma. Now, you've probably both been hearing one or two whispers about Kwok and Kwok and I wanted to let you know it's totally in hand and there's no need to worry.'

I look at Guy, who looks at me back and gives a little shrug.

'We've not heard any whispers, Tim,' I say to the phone. 'We've not heard anything at all about – what sort of whispers?'

No reply.

I wonder, fleetingly, if we've lost the connection since I hear not the confidently fluent accents of our son but the cries of birds. Guy leans towards the phone.

'Are you there, Tim?' he says.

'Sure, Pops! Well I shouldn't have jumped the gun, I guess, if you've heard nothing. Typical bloody Hong Kong! Echo chamber. Someone starts a story. You know – this firm isn't sound, that firm isn't sound – and it's everywhere in no time, and people get fidgety, and money stops flowing, blah blah blah. If you haven't heard anything, that's all good.'

He lets out a little laugh, a little bark.

'So you've called simply to tell us not to listen to the whispers and not to worry?' says Guy.

'Yip!'

'Well if that's all, then of course we won't worry. After all, you know about money, and we don't know about money.'

A second little bark.

'I sure do know about money. Okay, now that we've sorted that out I'd best be getting on with work. Ciao!'

'Bye, sweetheart,' I say, ending the call before looking up. 'It's lovely that he was so nice to my poor Guysie – I never heard he was kind.'

'Who?' says Guy, puzzling. 'Tim?'

'Bertie!'

'Oh, Bertie. Yes, he was kind. His kindness was only for the weak, I think. The weak, and the meek.'

'It takes all sorts, doesn't it?'

Guy says nothing. He looks away at the woodlands. I give him a little pat, the dear old darling. Although I'm not at all sure, between you and me, that I do think it takes all sorts. Or not his sort – Bertie's sort, I mean. Was he the sort of man who – well, you know what I mean – Bertie was – I can't help but feel he was somehow unsavoury.

We sit silently side-by-side for a bit, after which Guy begins speaking, very slowly, evidently needing to feel his way.

'What stays in my mind most about Bertie are a few words he spoke on his last day at Whitepark. He was packed and ready to go. He'd tied his hair into a ponytail and a light norwester was blowing down from the Alps. A blackbird was pecking through the nearest flowerbed. I loved watching birds then, just the way I love watching birds now. The blackbird was flicking up scraps of pea straw. The sky seemed very high above my small skull. It was a typical norwest sky, streaked with violet cirrus. Bertie stooped to me, bending low. He was a tall rangy fellow, so he had to bend very low.'

Guy, stopping, seems moved – though with him it's always hard to know.

'Yes, darling?' I prompt.

'He kissed my left cheek. The kiss was warm, and light. Nobody, so far as I knew, had kissed me ever since I'd been a baby. And he said something.'

I don't like what I'm hearing. It seems wrong.

Guy, stopping again, again looks away.

'What did he say?'

'I know you, Guy. We're the same, you and I.'

'Hmm, that's – interesting.' I say, though to be frank I think it shocking, somehow. 'Was he right, do you think?'

'I don't know. I wanted him to be right. I thought he was wrong. We weren't the same. He was odd. I was ordinary.'

CHAPTER FOUR

Guy and I look out the window. A wintry landscape. A low dark sky. Trees stripped down by the season of the year to corded strings, woody tendon. I hate winter, secretly. I hate winter because I want to be warm always. I hate winter because it makes me think that our planet doesn't care about us, doesn't care about anything. Well, how can it? It's a planet! It thinks nothing. It feels nothing. We're just wriggling around on top of a shallow scraping of soil, under a slight sheath of air, and above us is a vacuum, and below us is lava.

'Oh dear,' I say. 'Well at least we had those few days skiing at Coronet Peak.'

'And you'll have lots of fun tonight, Pwu.'

'We'll *both* have lots of fun! You'll let yourself take it easy, won't you? You'll forget about your books and your – well, you know, darling – your thoughts. You'll forget all that. You'll just let yourself enjoy the lovely food and the lovely wine and all our lovely friends and family, won't you? Please, Guysie?'

He smiles at me bravely but sort of sadly.

'Right you are.'

'Good boy. Now let's get into our glad rags!'

My glad rags, when I show them off for his approval two hours or so later, are a very simple frock of black silk. I've had it cut low over my plump bust. A diamond choker snug around my neck, with matching diamonds on my earlobes and wrists. My best diamonds, needless to say. As for Guy, it's only a matter of his best black dinner jacket.

'Gosh – dashing chap!' I say, lying. 'Aren't I the lucky one to have such a handsome husband?'

'I'm the lucky one, darling,' he says, also lying.

We wander into the dining room to survey the settings. Catering staff greet us smilingly. Swags of flowers in silver vessels. Silver candlesticks. The food tonight is going to be French, and not cuisine bourgeoise, either – haute cuisine only.

'Can't go wrong with haute cuisine, darling,' I said to Guy a week or two ago, knowing perfectly well that he really had no opinion and would have been quite happy with cheese and an apple or two. 'It's always correct.'

'Right you are, Pwu.'

We wander back into the sitting room nearest the front hallway. We sip sherry. We hear a car crunch to a halt on the gravel of the driveway.

'She's *unsound*!' we hear Jim booming out. 'Don't believe I've *ever* had a mare so unsound!'

'Lame, is she?' we hear from Harry Hall.

'Not lame, *vicious*. Stable vice. She's a bloody *kicker*, and a bloody *bolter*!'

Harry wears a dinner jacket. Jim has squeezed herself into a grotesque slip of silver silk that makes her look like a shiny strange stranded marine mammal. The two of them, while getting inside the house, keep talking.

'A bolter?' says Harry. 'Some saying about stable doors and horses bolting, isn't there?'

'Very *droll*, Harry,' hoots Jim.

Harry looks to be enough under the weather already to make me think he was speaking in honest perplexity.

'Eh?'

'She bolts her *feed*, Harry. I'll sell her to the works. She'll be bloody cat feed *herself*, if she doesn't mend her ways.'

Other guests turn up.

Cousins, friends. All our own generation, nobody old or young. Mummy and Daddy haven't come They've gone away, following the sun on a long holiday. As for my mother-in-law and father-in-law, that's an old story. Guy grew up on the Blandwood family property, Whitepark. A beautiful property. The house, though, is very cold. High wide rooms, hollow. The grounds are cold, too. Old trees, heavy and shady. My mother-in-law was a lean alert woman with big front teeth and very pale blue eyes and she absolutely adored driving at speed. She drove a gold Daimler. She swore by Daimlers. She swore by a lot of things. Also she was fiercely loyal to her dogs. German shepherds. Great Danes. She never had time for small dogs.

'Can't bear little damn *yappers*,' she used to say.

My mother-in-law was driving, recklessly as always, one day seven years ago. Alongside her, smoking a pipe, was my father-in-law. A crossroads. A truck, laden with a load of lambs, bound for the freezing works. Sunstrike. The medical opinion afterwards was that neither my mother-in-law nor my father-in-law would have felt any pain. Nor did my poor boy seem to feel any pain, though he was hiding it, most likely, hiding it away.

He was taught from when he was a tot to keep his upper lip stiff.

As, of course, was I.

A winter party. A fire of blue gum logs, though only for show. We have very good central heating. Cousins and friends looking about, eyes dimmed faintly by the years, lips thinned by those same years, teeth whitened by dentists. Costly suits. Costly frocks. A lithe young waiter padding back and forth with drinks on a silver tray. Cousins and friends chatting.

'Who was that chap who – ?'

'Going like a rudderless bat out of hell – '

'A very nice muscley chestnut thoroughbred, though prone to jib – '

Guy, slipping over to me at one point, murmurs that it might be an idea to phone the offs before we sit down to table. Otherwise, he adds, they're likely to ring at a time that might be a bit awkward. We both know, but don't say, that neither of the kids is likely to ring at all and that our taking the first step is the only way we can be sure to get birthday greetings. We go through to the quiet blue emptiness of the library. The books are in darkness. The oxblood sofas seem to be brooding. The French windows show us a vacant night sky.

Guy and I stand next to the loo table. I key in a number for Tim. Guy begins spinning the old globe. He spins it idly, playing a game he often plays. Closing his eyes, reaching out with his right index finger, he touches the globe's surface at random and then opens his eyes to see where the finger has landed.

I look, listening to the sound of the phone ringing, at the spot he lands on now.

A bit of empty space near Rio de Janeiro.

Tim turns out to be busy. I try Charley. She answers straightaway. I put her on to loudspeaker as she begins gabbling.

'Mummy! Papa! Happy Birthday, darlings! So, so wish I was there with you. Sorry, so, so – oh blimey, what was I wanting to say? I'm a bit disrevelled – '

'Disrevelled, darling?' I reply.

'Totally, Mummy! – you know, busy busy – big shoot yesterday and big night last night – and today a new shoot for *The Lady* – leisure wear, to use the jargon – the look for this summer – honestly, though, I'm not feeling so very summery – wish I could be back home with you, darlings –the delicious frosts and things – and – and, to be perfectly honest, darlings, I'm not feeling totally wonderful right now – no, Mummy, nothing serious, course not – no, only I – well, darlings, it's just – I mean, darlings, everything's fab, goes without saying – everything's totally fab – but I mean to say is – is – you know, darlings? I mean, really – though as I say, a touch disrevelled this morning – out jolloping last night – and, well you know me and how I do adore to jollop – perhaps a little too much, haha – anyway, darlings, what was I saying?'

The globe spinning.

A spot in the ocean near Tahiti.

The slang can be tricky but standard sentences have never been characteristic of Charley.

'Lovely to hear your voice, sweetheart,' I say, winding up. 'Now, sadly, I suppose we'd better get back to our guests.'

The globe –

Samarkand.

Yet those sentences today seem even less standard than ordinarily.

'Oh! Oh, yes, course, darlings – course you must get back to your guests – your guests are so important, aren't they? – oh yes, you must get back to them, mustn't you? – why waste your precious time talking to your kid? – after all, she's only your baby girl – yes, darlings – forget about your little girl, won't you?'

Guy flicks me an unhappy look.

'Charley, darling,' I try, 'is something wrong?'

'Sorry, sorry, sorry Mummy! – don't mean to be a bitch – course you must get back to everybody – it's your special day, darlings! – as I say, everything's fab – you two have heaps and heaps and heaps of fun, that's an order, darlings! – and now – kisses, sweethearts – kisses Mummy – kisses Papa – I'd better run myself, too – bye bye! – bye bye!'

Guy and I look at each other, wondering.

'Well, what was that about?' I try.

'She's always been rather up and down, darling, hasn't she?'

'Yes, but – well, we'd better get back to everybody.'

Our friends and cousins are still at it, drinking and talking and drinking.

'I'm afraid that's rather wide of the mark, in my opinion,' someone says to somebody. 'What I'd say about the matter would be – '

'Wonder why we call them sitting rooms when at a do like this we stand up?' says somebody to someone. 'Or does it only occur to me to wonder because I've already had two snifters of this excellent sherry?'

I move about, nodding, smiling, laughing, confiding. Guy moves about, too, though less smoothly. Happy birthday, I'm thinking. A birthday isn't a very logical thing to celebrate, when you think about it, given that the baby when squeezed out of the womb is already a fully formed being who's been feeling and thinking for some months in its cosy rosy darkness before finding itself suddenly shoved out into a world of hot and cold, light and night. A more logical thing to celebrate, perhaps, would be the day of conception; though that in itself presupposes that being conceived, coming into being, is in itself something worth celebrating.

'We'll go through now,' I say to everybody.

'Right,' they say.

Cousins and friends, friends and cousins, downing the last of their drinks, troop after me into a dining room glowing now with newly lighted candles and winking with small stars on the bowls of silver spoons and the tines of silver forks. I, helped by the meagre arm of our very slothful cousin Quentin Tancred, go to my place at the head of the table. Guy, taking the muscled arm of our very sporty cousin Cynthia Locke-Luxmoore, goes to his place at the bottom of the table. Jim seats herself in her spot next to Quentin.

The waiters start ladling out soup.

Three tureens, each with a different soup.

'I hear you've come into something left to you by batty old Bertie Blandwood,' says Quentin. 'A bit of property in – where is it? Fiji?'

'Samoa,' I say mildly.

'Very nice,' says Quentin. 'You'll sell it up, I suppose?'

'Actually, in point of fact we've made up our minds to go over there and – '

'*Ber*tie!' butts in Jim. 'He was a *character* if ever there was a bloody character!'

'Never met him myself,' says Quentin. 'Why was he thought so scandalous?'

'Rubbed everyone the wrong way,' I reply.

Jim lets out a guffaw.

'*Curry* combed everyone the wrong way!' she shouts. 'After *filing* the *teeth* of the comb!'

Jim happens to have been the only one of us around the table who ever saw Bertie from any point of view other than that of a little girl or boy. She was in her teens when he came home to stay on his last fraught holiday.

'How?' asks Quentin. 'What sort of thing?'

A long string of short sentences now follows, barked out happily by Jim. He was rum, she says. He wasn't what you come upon among our crowd. He wore his hair very long. He talked about the Buddha. His wrists jangled with brass bangles. He talked about nuclear disarmament and social democracy. He wore loose baggy shirts dyed citron yellow and lime green and parrot red. He said our land wasn't our land but belonged by right to everybody. He said we were stamped from one dull mould and needed to do some hard thinking and find who we were really.

'He said we had even more of a mob instinct than our *sheep*!' whoops Jim.

'Hmm,' says Quentin. 'Chip on his shoulder?'

'He was a kind man,' I say.

Aware that my only warrant for those words is Guy, yet not knowing what else to say to gag Quentin, let alone an always ungaggable Jim. Waiters are topping up wineglasses. I chose the wines carefully from the vineyards I like best in Marlborough, Canterbury and Otago. Afterwards, the waiters whisk away our soup bowls and bring around hors d'oeuvre.

Roquefort and pear quiche, and buttered snails.

'You two bloody well *can't* go to Samoa!' raps out Jim. 'Go there and you'll go *troppo* on us!'

'Well as it happens we've never been to the tropics, other than the odd stopover at Singapore,' I reply. 'We talked it through and made up our minds to scratch Europe altogether this year and instead take a look at Paradise in Heaven.'

'Paradise in – what?' says Quentin.

'Paradise in Heaven, the estate Guy's been devised by Bertie. An estate in Samoa. At first I kept saying the estate had been bequeathed to Guy. He set me right and told me bequeath – you know, the verb – only pertains to personal, not real, property.'

'Paradise in Heaven!' says Quentin. 'Isn't it a – you know, what's the word?'

'A tautology?'

'That's the one!'

'I don't imagine it was given its name by Bertie. As you know, Blandwoods aren't noted for wasting words. We only got news of the estate a few days ago. The wheels of law take some time to spin, seemingly, in Samoa.'

'I should imagine every wheel takes some time to spin in such a sleepy hollow,' says Quentin. 'Lucky sods.'

'We're told the property is freehold, which is good because apparently most land is owned tribally in Samoa. Twenty or so hectares, right on the seafront.'

'Very nice.'

'We couldn't get hold of a schedule of improvements but there's a house and no doubt everything else needful. The house, I suppose, will be a bungalow. Open to the sea breeze, sort of style. I've got a clear picture of it in my head. A veranda on the ground floor. Upstairs, a balcony. Palm trees nodding and swaying. Also, of course, a sandy cove and a turquoise lagoon. Guy says he doesn't imagine I'm too far wrong. Bertie had his eccentricities but evidently liked his comforts, too.'

'As we all do,' says Quentin. 'And rightly so.'

'At first we thought it made sense just to sell the property, but that seemed somehow disrespectful to Bertie's memory. And that very hard frost the other day helped us make up our minds to go out on a bit of a limb.'

'Good for the *root* crops, though,' bays Jim.

'What?' I say. 'Sorry, Jim, I don't quite follow.'

'That *frost*, Pru! That frost was *bloody* good for the root crops!'

'We've not got any root crops in this winter,' observes Quentin, 'but the frost certainly was what was wanted for the rose garden and in my opinion we could do with a few more quite as sharp.'

'*Couldn't* agree more, Quent! A good stiff *fortnight* or two of frost would do our place splendidly!'

The weather, the paddocks, the stock, the slackness of staff, the foibles and follies of friends and cousins not at the dinner party, now follow one another as topics to be talked over by Jim and Quentin. My task is to make agreeable noises, mostly. Waiters, having loped away with the platters from which we chose our hors d'oeuvre, keep coming back with wine and, when the time is right, take away our plates. Afterwards they come back with the next course. My phone rings just as we pick up knives and forks.

'Guy,' I mouth silently, waving at him way down at the bottom of the table. 'Tim!''

Apologising to the guests, who beam and nod at us affectionately, we again go through to the library. Tim, when we start talking, turns out to have forgotten it's our birthday.

'Oops, bad son and all that sort of thing, Ma!' he burbles. 'I'm a bit squippy!'

'Squippy?'

'Yah!'

'Squippy, meaning – ?'

'Anyway, don't believe a word of it, about Kwok and Kwok. Kwok and Kwok are, like – I mean, the crap you might be hearing, it's total tosh!'

'Tosh?'

'Absolutely!'

The conversation goes around in several meaningless circles before he recalls the occasion and yaps out his hopes that we have a happy birthday.

'Thanks, Tim,' says Guy a bit cursorily. 'Look, can you tell us why you keep alluding to Kwok and Kwok – '

Click.

'Hung up?' I say.

'Well after all he's squippy.'

Quentin and Jim, when I get back to my seat, prove to be having a go at the latest harebrained tricks of the Labour government. They dwell on the flaws of the prime minister, Helen Clark. Admittedly she's clever, the prime minister. Yet wrongheaded, and smug. Her government has just brought in a dole for mothers of children aged three and four. The dole will allow them to pack their little ones off to some nursery school or other. Really it's not a lot better than baby farming. I mean, naturally every mother does wish for a bit of a break, now and then. But still, a break isn't what we're talking about here. The government's now going to give each of those women enough money to shirk their responsibilities for twenty hours every week, all year. And next year, too. Which, thank heaven, is an election year!

'What sort of mother,' asks Quentin, 'would hand her kids over to a motley crew of – well, mercenaries, frankly – people doing the work for the sake of the money – at one of those so-called childcare centres?'

'*Nanny* state!' trumpets Jim. 'Trust those *red* clowns for social engineering!'

A wreckage of plates gets whisked off by waiters, after which we have a choice of three desserts.

I ask for a bavarois. Jim takes a tarte tatin. Quentin goes for the Paris-Brest.

'As I was *saying*, Quen,' yaps a now cheerily legless Jim, 'spot of *trouble* in the hack paddock to sort out – '

The cheeses have been brought to table before either of my companions thinks to say anything more about Samoa.

'I can't help but envy you two, off to sun yourselves in the tropics,' says Quentin, driving a knife deep into a brie de Meaux. 'Myself, I'm just sticking to the tried and true.'

'The Rhineland?' I say.

'Mm,' answers Quentin. 'Good brie.'

'I'm the one who's keen,' I say. 'Guy had to be talked into it.'

'Really?' says Quentin. 'The brie?'

'Samoa,' I reply.

I talked him into it that morning of hard frost when we were walking together, wading in wool, our ears, noses and lips numb with cold. Distress signals of white vapour were puffing from our mouths.

'Let's go to Samoa,' I said, pumping gloved fists in and out of my pockets. 'I mean – maybe it's meant to be, Guysie?'

Guy looked at me almost sternly.

'What? How can we just – go? We know nothing about Samoa. Nobody goes there, Pwu. Nobody we know.'

'All the more reason for *us* to go!'

'We can't just go sight unseen, can we? We need to get in touch with people, the right people. We need to know what's what. We need to know everything. We need to know the ins and the outs of the property. We need to see photos. We need to see a video. We can't just get on a plane and jump into the deep end.'

'Yes we can – we've never jumped into the deep end. Let's do it for once – now!'

'A lot could go wrong, Pwu.'

'What could go wrong? We know there's a house. You've been bequeathed the property.'

'Devised the property.'

'And it's only a hop, skip and jump from here, really – isn't it? Quite close, anyway. I mean – well, I don't exactly know how far it is, but only an hour or two, I suppose?'

'I don't know. I suppose so.'

'We can pop over there quite lightheartedly – and – and if we turn out not to have been dealt trumps we can just – well, we can just jolly well come straight back home again! We'll do it lightheartedly – and we'll travel light. We need to learn how to travel light. We always work things out too much in advance – we always plan everything for ages in advance – and that's not the way to live, really, is it? And that's why things are always disappointing. The birthday party will be disappointing. I know it's going to be disappointing because I've been looking forward to it so much, so I warrant you it'll be disappointing. I mean – the trick to enjoying life must be just to do things for the hell of it, don't you think? Doing a thing at the moment you want to do a thing. Yes, darling?'

'No, darling,' he answered gently.

'Yes, Guysie! I mean, we're always so sensible – always so – so fucking sensible!'

'Are we so fucking sensible?' he said teasingly.

I suddenly burst out laughing.

'Yes, darling, we're always so fucking fucking – *fucking* – sensible! I want to do something rash.'

'Rash? A dangerous new doctrine, Prudence.'

'Hah – you mean yes! Yes, that's what you mean, isn't it?'

'Yes.'

Quentin is now droning on about something that happened to him when he was a boy at College. Jim is knocking back a port. I feel sleepy. The birthday party will end only after the speeches, and the toasts, and our friends and cousins singing a song telling us we're jolly good fellows, and more drinks, and more talk, and more drinks, and so on and so forth, until at last we'll shut the front door for the last time that night and the last cars will roll away down the driveway.

I glance down the table at Guy.

I grin broadly.

Samoa!

Part 2: CHAPTER FIVE

Not too nasty, this wine. I roll a mouthful between my tongue and palate. Dry, a slight taste of greywacke and, perhaps, gooseberry? Anyway, near enough for business class. I swallow the mouthful slowly. The trip has taken a lot longer than we'd supposed. Quite a lot more than three hours. A bit tedious. Not that business class is so very awful. I've got a white leather seat, a white leather footrest and a little low table thingy.

At one point, feeling bored – before telling a stewardess I wanted my third glass of wine – I counted the seats.

Twenty-four, of which fifteen are holding nothing but thin air. Or in other words there's only nine of us, nine people. A couple of slight Chinese chaps in spivvy suits. They must be something to do with money. A big Samoan woman in a big brown jacket. A quartet of big Samoan men in big black jackets.

Also me, roly-poly little me, sitting by my window.

Oh yes, also, to my left, Guy.

'We'll be beginning our descent soon, bishop,' says a stewardess, stooping to one of the four big Samoan men. 'Please buckle up.'

I saw the bishop at the airport, ambling slowly on heavy feet while wearing a black lavalava and gripping a carved stick. A lavalava is the sort of skirt they wear, a sort of sarong. I know because I've been swotting up. Tagging along in the bishop's wake was a young fellow in trackpants who said nothing and lugged the cabin bags.

Golly, *beginning our descent*. Our descent to –

A tropical paradise!

I suppose it goes with the job for a bishop to wear black but what a pity he's not wearing wonderful colour. Samoans love colour, don't they? You know, the kind of bright, hot colour I can't get away with. Guy, all those years ago on our wedding day, said my skin was like silk. Now it's like wallpaper. Flocked wallpaper. Stuck on with paste. Will it melt in the heat in Samoa?

'Guysie,' I say, turning to my left a tad tipsily. 'They'll be very – you know, simple and so on, won't they?'

He knits his brow.

'Who, Pwu?'

'The Samoans. They'll be so alive, darling. Alive – and alert – and – and happy.'

'I assume we'll encounter what one finds anywhere and everywhere,' he says with a sort of sad creased smile. 'The standard mixed assortment of humanity.'

Poor old Guy. The wine hasn't gone to his head. He never lets it, the silly boy. He's had his statutory two glasses.

'No, they'll be lovely, Guysie. You know – soulful, and sweet and – and in touch with nature!'

Once more the sad creased smile.

'Right you are, Pwu.'

Now the stewardess is bending towards me, reaching out.

'We're nearly ready for our descent, madam. Shall I take your wineglass?'

'Must you?' I say.

She must. Even when you come on an adventure you've still got to do things properly. Doing things properly. Story of my life. I hand over the glass. I look out my window. A paradise, certifiably a paradise, is gliding up towards the glass. Green islands. Coral reefs. White surf. Tiny houses. Tiny streets, crisscrossing. The people down there must be steamy, simmering under the sun, sheltering under the shade of roofs thatched from things like the fronds of coconut palm. People – brown people – thinking things, feeling things, so unlike anything we feel, or think.

Intriguing, exciting –

Uncanny!

Now the two main islands are sprawling away to either side, clouds hiding their jungled peaks. Upolu on one side. Savai'i on the other side. We're dropping lower and lower towards Upolu. White sands. Green lagoons. A ragged range of those jungled peaks.

The rumble of the landing gear.

Palm trees leaping up towards us – the airport – the runway. We're dropping, dropping. The shriek of the jets.

We land with a bang.

'Welcome to Samoa,' says a voice over the intercom. 'Fa'afeiloai i Samoa.'

Guy and I are soon stepping down the gangway, walking across the tarmac, shading our eyes and looking around edgily. Samoans sail slowly onwards, heads back. Glass doors, a little dingy, slide open into a tiny immigration hall. A booth for Samoan nationals. A booth for diplomats and special needs. Two booths for foreigners.

We're foreigners, of course.

Funny to think we once owned this place, it was our colony, and now we're foreigners and have to stand in a queue behind the businessmen from China. A young woman in a cheap white shirt looks at me blankly as I step up to a booth. A solid young woman. Well, they all seem to be pretty solid, don't they? Samoans. Shiny black hair scraped back and plaited to one side. Shiny round face, rather flat. A pair of big brown eyes. She could – with a touch of lipstick, a little eyeshadow – be quite pretty.

Help, my first contact with a Samoan!

I boost my smile wattage.

'Do you speak English?' I say, meaning to be careful and slow, but somehow it comes out as a slurred gush.

Ooops – I really am a bit tight!

The girl, nodding uninterestedly, holds out a rather massive mitt for my passport.

'What a lovely country you have! My first time here! So looking forward to it! Do the coconuts up in those trees out there ever drop on anybody? So hot, isn't it? Sticky! Is the air conditioning not working? All in order with my passport? You do speak English don't you?'

I'm blithering.

Not a word, meanwhile, from the young woman. A thump of a rubber stamp. A curt nod. Not a nice way to welcome newcomers to your country, really.

Yet somehow I feel I'm on the back foot. I stop, to wait for Guy. A woman about my age stands nearby. Samoan. She's wearing a long loose dress patterned with brown and orange swirls and her mighty feet have been stuffed inside nylon socks – pink and sparkly – and the socks have been stuffed, in turn, into red slippers. Her greying hair has been scraped up into a topknot.

Odd, isn't it?

Odd that she and I are about the same age yet she's her and I'm me. How does it happen? I mean, how does it happen that we get born – you know, all of us – how does it happen that she gets born here, and I get born elsewhere, and everything about us grows out of that? I mean, in a sense we could be the same woman. Yet in another sense, she's an utter mystery. What's going on inside that big heavy skull, below that stringy topknot? And, for her, I must be just as much a mystery.

Why do things work out one way and not another way?

And can we choose?

Well, no, of course we can't choose. We're born and we grow up and that's about it, really, isn't it? I mean, we're what our home country and our childhood and our family and our schools, and all the rest of it – we're what those things make us, aren't we? We can't choose anything, really.

Can we?

Waiting, wondering about the ins and outs, I look through to the baggage hall where young men are singing some sort of native ditty, not strikingly well. The boys look agreeable, though a bit scruffy.

What a very funny little place this is!

'Cooee, darling,' says Guy, coming alongside. 'Penny for them?'

'Mmm? Just getting my bearings, sweetheart.'

The baggage hall is hot and dark. The conveyor belt hasn't started conveying. I feel not right, somehow. Aren't we supposed to be welcomed by pretty girls coming forward and throwing leis around our necks, and everybody smiling, and laughing, and speaking in musical tones, while the scent of a thousand tropical blooms wafts through the air, and boys in light yellow and frangipani and cerulean shirts come hurrying up to us wanting to whisk our bags away?

'I do so hope the house has a pool,' I say to Guy. 'I'm awfully in need of feeling cool.'

'I'm pretty sure it'll have a pool.'

Our bags pop up on the belt and still no boys to do the whisking, so we set ourselves to the task of a bit of heave-ho. We're travelling light, luckily. Apia, after all. Not quite Florence or Paris. Not likely we'll need evening dress! I did cram in one little Karen Walker black frock, just in case we get asked along to some do or other hosted by the High Commission. And two strings of my better pearls. Otherwise, linen skirts, cotton and silk blouses, a few pair of strappy sandals. My makeup bag. No stockings. My stash of Anita Brookner and Muriel Spark. Two sets of swimming togs.

'Now, taxi,' says Guy. 'And then the house.'

'And the pool,' I add.

I see myself, an hour so from now, floating in our pool. I'm wearing my dove grey togs. Only, somehow, they've become a vivid scarlet. At the side of the pool, smiling, is one of the house staff. A girl or boy, glistening with sweat, holding out a gin and tonic on a silver tray. The sunshine strikes the silver and shoots rays of happiness into my eye.

Wine is lovely but nothing, after all, beats a gin and tonic.

Guy and I, each pushing a trolley, make our way to the green lane for our customs declaration. Afterwards, out we go to the arrivals concourse where we find masses of people – dark, laborious people – milling about in a sultry sort of cave. A lot of picaninnies are running to and fro, some with noses streaming. A cluster of youths in shapeless shorts are leaning against a soiled concrete column. Old women are looking on dourly. The only person smiling is a cabbie seeking customers, a scrawny man in a yellow shirt and green lavalava.

'You wanna tassi?'

His massive legs, below the frayed hem of the green lavalava, are badly scarred. I wonder why.

'Oh,' I answer, looking around for Guy. 'Ah – one moment, please.'

Guy, having stopped short, is gaping at the whole scene with barely suppressed dismay. I take one step towards him. He takes one faltering step towards me. I want, suddenly, to grab his hand, trot straight back through the baggage hall, and the immigration hall, and up the steps into the safety of Air New Zealand. I do no such thing, of course, because after all – well, I'm a grown woman, a mother, a freeholder, a ratepayer, a taxpayer, a registered elector, a committee member, a member of vestry. Running away simply isn't a possibility, is it? Stepping forward, striding forward, is the right thing to do, isn't it? Or so they say. I think the only time I strode forward – other, perhaps, than while racketing around Europe after getting my degree – was when I was thirteen at St Margaret's. I owned up to my form mistress, Miss Francey, that I was the culprit who'd written *Miss Fanny* on the blackboard.

I knew it was the right thing to do, to own up.

Miss Francey gave me a thousand lines.

'Guysie, what do you think? This chap's offering a taxi. Do you think it's safe to say yes?'

Ordinarily we'd have booked a car, and we'd calmly be keeping an eye cocked for a driver holding up a card, but our travel agent back home told us we could get away without booking. Not booking? We found the idea rather charming.

'We'd better have a bit of a powwow, Pwu.'

'Right, yes.'

'I mean – are there licensed taxis?'

I turn back to the man with scarred legs and say something about not yet being ready. He slouches away. Guy and I go into a scrum of two. We quickly work out that we both thought we'd find an orderly queue somewhere, with porters ready to take charge of baggage and clean cars waiting in a row. What we see instead is disarray inside and, outside, a welter of dubious wheeled objects. How can we know which driver can be trusted, which chassis is warranted?

We push our trolleys outside to take a survey.

The sun flares like a million diamonds. Diamonds cut by some manic jeweller into cruel, sharp shapes. We stumble to the shade of a concrete overhang. We catch sight of a taxi rank and, seated on the kerb, a man who seems to be a driver. A burly young man wearing a white shirt and black lavalava. He catches our eye.

'Whadda yous guys looking for?'

I'm not used to being addressed as one of yous guys. Of course I know I shouldn't feel upset, but I am. Also I feel nervous about what he wants, what he's seeing. He's not seeing me the way I'm used to being seen, seemingly.

Is he seeing through me?

'We need a taxi to take us to a place near Apia,' says Guy. 'A place called Paradise in Heaven.'

He shakes his head.

'Dunno that place.'

'You are a taxi driver though?' presses on Guy.

'Yeah, but not working right now.'

'Why not?' I cut in, a little too sharply.

'Feeling lazy right now,' he says, leaning back his big body, lifting his big strong arms and cradling his big happy head in the palms of his big strong hands.

I feel a mixture of irritation, fear and envy.

'What?' I snap.

'Someone come along soon,' says the young man peaceably.

What does he mean, someone will come along? Who? When? How can a taxi driver not want a fare? Guy and I fidget back and forth along the concrete platform until in the end the lazy cabbie, taking pity, calls over one of his friends who says that for fifty tala he can drive us to anywhere in or near Apia. The friend is another burly young man wearing a white shirt and black lavalala. Fifty tala is about thirty dollars. We say yes. The burly young man heaves our bags into the boot. We step into his taxi, an old dented Datsun whose vinyl upholstery has been split by years of backsides and heat. A cardboard cutout of Christ bleeds luridly below the rearview mirror. The driver starts the motor. Samoan pop music blasts from the radio.

'You here on holiday?' says the driver.

'Yes,' we both reply at the same time. 'On holiday.'

'Snap, darling!' says Guy, squeezing my elbow in a fraught way.

'Can we have the air conditioning? I say.

'Don't work,' says the driver.

Tired, hot, sticky, we sit inside a creaking squeaking steel box while a tarry road burrows through a ratty landscape. Coconut palms, banana trees. Shanties, shops – little rickety shops. Women and men dawdling. Youngsters, and rangy dogs, and small black pigs. The driver pulls up in front of a lopsided shop. We huddle on the back seat while an endless sort of yarning begins, heaven knows why, between him and some young fellow.

'Well, darling, they say that on the islands people don't live by the clock,' I try gamely. 'Quite fun really, isn't it?'

'Mm, lots more fun than being back at home in front of the fire with a cup of tea and a copy of *Forest and Bird*.'

I shoot out a short laugh, perhaps a trifle hysterically.

'And some scrummy yumyums! For our tumtums!'

'Yes, Pwupwu.'

'Oh, and after the yumyums, Guysie, two or three rumrums!'

Off we creak and squeak once more, burrowing onwards through a tunnel of tree trunks, a runnel of rubbish, a village, a tangled wilderness, another village, yet another village. Bungalows, rusted and ramshackle or sometimes freshly painted and slick. Other houses – most houses – have no walls, they're no more than floors from which pillars sprout, topped by hipped roofs. Plastic chairs, boxes, cans, cotton cloth printed with hibiscus, woven matting. Old people sit staring at shifting shapes on television while young mothers hold newborns or whack toddlers.

I feel anxious.

I don't know how to manage this country.

Can this be real? Do people really live like this? Is this what the whole of Samoa is like? Or is this a particularly poor tract of territory?

'I totally forgot the place,' says the driver. 'You say near Apia?'

'Paradise in Heaven,' says Guy.

'Where that?'

'A bay about eight kilometres from Apia. I don't know the name of the bay, or the village.'

'I ask,' says the driver.

We stop shortly outside another lopsided shop. Guy and I, while the driver goes inside, look at each other wonderingly.

'Surely he'd know without needing to ask?' I try. 'Given what we've seen already, there can't be too many houses here on the scale of Paradise in Heaven.'

'Perhaps he's not a local, Pwu.'

'Darling, going by the – well, poverty – of these villages, I'd say Paradise in Heaven must be famous throughout the whole of Samoa. The driver may be trying to cheat us by taking a roundabout way.'

'He charged us a flat fee though, darling.'

'He looks sly.'

'I think our first lesson today, Pwu, must be that nothing's necessarily what it seems in Samoa.'

The driver slopes out of the shop , dumps himself behind the wheel, tells us we're not far away, grinds into gear, and off we go. A lawyer who spoke to us by phone on behalf of the estate said that while it may not seem orthodox for us simply to bowl up at Paradise in Heaven without untying any red tape in Apia, that's the way things are in this neck of the woods. All we need to do, he went on to say, is find a fellow who lives on the property. A fellow going by the startling moniker of Stevenson Bismarck. He was, evidently, Bertie's right-hand-man.

'I can almost taste that first gin and tonic,' I say.

We turn a bend on an earthen road and come upon yet another village amidst rooting pigs and black lava lumps. Listless waves slap in a lagoon. The unlucky dwellers of this wretched spot are blessed with no sandy beach or groves of coconut. Our road halts at a patch of savannah grass, coarse and sharp, in the midst of which a weathered wooden deck sits on posts. A thatched roof above the deck looks like a broken umbrella.

'This it,' says the driver, grinding down the gears and stopping.

The man's got himself lost, in other words.

'No,' says Guy. 'We're looking for Paradise in Heaven.'

'This it,' repeats the driver. 'Just only this – first time I hear that name – but this it.'

He points to a wooden plank, cracked by long years of sun, painted with three worn red words in a manner one can only call slapdash. *Paradise in Heaven*, says the plank unconvincingly. Clearly there must be two places with the same name on this godforsaken island. Guy and I, after stiffly climbing out of the cab, hold another quick powwow. We agree to try to find someone in the village who might know where we should be going. As we peer about, the bleached door of what seems to be a privy swings open on a man. A scowling sinewy man with a closely scalped skull.

'Who the hell are you!' he shouts.

Guy, straightening his already straight back, steps forward in what I think of as his hail-fellow-well-met manner, which comes very hard to him.

'Guy Blandwood,' he says slowly, 'nephew of the late Bertram Blandwood.'

The man keeps scowling.

'Who?'

Guy speaks still more slowly.

'Guy Bland-wood, ne-phew of Ber-tram Bland-wood.'

'Not here!'

Guy begins to speak what I imagine he fancies is Pidgin.

'We looking place him name Paradise in Heaven, him belong Mr Blandwood. Him house anywhere near here?'

The man keeps scowling.

Welts, a row of welts – pink and white – pockmark the back of his noggin. Welts that look slightly sickening. Scabs from some nasty tropical disease, very likely. Contagious? I must be eyeing the welts too obviously since I now get a scowl of my own from the man.

'Machete!' he snaps.

'Oh, er – '

'Machete chopped me!' he keeps snapping. 'Chop, chop, chop!'

He steps towards me, waving an arm in the air. I think he's making the movement of someone striking machete blows. I step back. Oh for that gin and tonic! I'm hot. I'm drunk. I'm sweaty. I'm sleepy. Guy, stepping forward, tries talking to the man. The man is still shouting. The man is waving his hands. The man is shouting louder and louder, and looking pretty threatening.

My phone rings.

'Pru, *had* to call! How's Samoa? You'll never *believe* the latest move by bloody Buffy!'

'Sorry, can't talk, Jim. A bit of a situation here. We're crossing swords.'

'Crossing swords? You and *Guy*?'

'Don't be silly, you know he and I are always the best of friends. No, we're lost in some wilderness. A villager is throwing something of a fit. Not altogether sure why.'

'Go straight for the *jugular*, Pru!'

'Whose jugular, Jim? I don't quite follow.'

'Whoever you're crossing *swords* with over there in Samoa.'

'Oh, he's – well, he's just some fellow.'

'*Straight* for the jugular, Pru!'

'Will do, Jim.'

'I'll hove off. Will fill you in *later* about Buffy.'

I hear a pitter-patter behind me, and children tittering, and dogs barking, and a pig squealing. I swivel on the spot. A ragtag mob of urchins have come running towards me, grinning. Ragtag and dirty. I start to fix a smile on my face, ready to say a few sugary things to sweeten the situation, since clearly they're excited to see a real live white woman in their benighted land of the lost.

Thwack!

Ow!

What was that? It hurts! I reel. I put my hand to my forehead. Ow! Ow ow ow! One of those little brutes has thrown a stone! They're giggling. One of them grabs something from the road and flings it. Another stone! It whisks past me.

What the hell are these filthy little brats – ?

A big brown man – our driver – looms up on my left, pounds past, shouts something. He's shooing the brats away. They turn tail. He boots one or two in the backside. My fingertips, meanwhile, feel sticky. Taking them away, I'm stunned to see they're red with blood. *My* blood!

Should I have had a tetanus booster before coming to Samoa?

What other infections, besides tetanus, can one catch from a soiled stone in a village oinking with pigs?

My upbringing kicks in.

Keep calm, Pru. Just breathe deeply. You're a Tancred. Apia will have antibiotics. The airport is only an hour away. Two or three or flights a day to New Zealand. Lifting my chin – partly to stop the blood dripping into my mouth – I start walking towards the shade of a big tree, a big sprawling tree, a tree I soon understand is a breadfruit. I've never seen a breadfruit tree before, but I know what it is because when doing my swot for our trip I looked at pics of the fruit and the leaves, and it's very green and very shiny and very fresh and rather magnificent.

I take my deep breaths, slowly.

What's that, just behind the tree trunk?

Something rather sweet. A wooden cross. A posy of fresh flowers twisted together with what looks like coconut twine. A framed photo. Stooping – which unluckily has the effect of making the blood flow from my forehead more freely – I see that the photo shows two people, a man and a woman. The man is the man who just came out of the privy. He's kissing the woman. A white woman of about sixty. A blowsy woman. A blowsy woman with a big beehive hairdo, dyed red, lacquered, skewered with a yellow hibiscus. The woman could do with a new hairdresser and a few tips on makeup. And a new dressmaker, given that she's swathed her scrawny breasts inside a violet lavalava, tucked under hairy armpits!

Yet the woman, for all her vulgarity, looks extraordinarily happy.

As does the man.

I look at the photo wonderingly. Very hard to grasp that the man who came scowling out of the privy and who's still shouting at poor Guy is the same man kissing with eager warmth at that raddled and – well, tarty – woman. His kiss, and his eyes, seem not only warm but somehow – glowing. And the woman, too – she, too, seems to glow.

Love, that's what I'm seeing.

Love.

I feel lonely.

Guy scuffs across the springy grass to my side.

'He says we've got the wrong place, darling. He's very emphatic about it. He says – '

He stops.

His eyes boggle.

'Yes, darling?' I prompt. 'He says – ?'

'Bertie!' yelps Guy, gaping at the photo under glass.

The heat must be getting to the poor boy. The stress. I'd better take charge, clearly.

'Bertie?' I prompt a little more quietly, aware that I myself am now almost tempted to lapse into some sort of Pidgin. 'What about Bertie?'

'That photo. The – person – on the left in that photo is – well, it's Uncle Bertie.'

My turn to boggle.

The person on the left is the blowsy woman.

CHAPTER SIX

The sweaty space inside the taxi swells with the sound of a church choir – a native choir singing hymns over the radio – as the driver, following our orders, wheels around and begins to bump and bounce back towards the sealed road. Guy, meanwhile, takes a turn on the phone. We've brought only the one phone along on this trip because neither of us likes managing a lot of gadgets. Our laptops we've left at home, too.

Guy dials the lawyer in Apia, waits for a bit, hangs up.

'Engaged, Guysie?'

'Not even a recorded message, Pwu.'

We bounce. We bump. Guy fiddles about with the phone, does some keying, peers at the screen nearsightedly. I look out the window. Houses on posts. Hungry dogs. Hens pecking in grass. We get to the main road, We turn towards Apia. The radio hymns give way to the quacking of some American missionary. He's talking about the Mystery of the Shawl. I've never in my life as an observing Anglican ever heard anyone say anything about any Mystery of the Shawl. Moses, or so says the missionary, after the flight from Egypt was told by God that all the sons of Israel – not the daughters, evidently – had to wear a shawl with tassels, specifically one tassel on each of the four corners, to show the will of the Lord. Or did the missionary say the word of the Lord?

'You'd better press your handkerchief harder on that graze, darling,' says Guy. 'It's starting to drip again.'

'Oh bother! I'll need to soak this hanky in cold water the moment we check in – wherever it is we're checking in!'

'The phone says the best place to stay is Queen Lupe's Hotel.'

'Do you think we'd better drop in on the lawyer before we try to find ourselves somewhere to stay?'

'Your guess is as good as mine, darling. Let's get ourselves a couple of rooms and a cup of tea, and get that wound of yours bathed and dressed. We could speak to the police at some point after that, too.'

'The police? Why? You think that awful man back there is a squatter or something?'

'No no, not that. I was thinking we need to report the boy who threw the stone.'

'Oh he's just a kid. No point, really. As for the cup of tea, I think for myself I'll be wanting something with a bit more kick.'

'Right you are, Pwu.'

I'm not game to say anything about that sordid spot stuck amidst the rooting pigs, that nowhere, that nothingness, our Paradise in Heaven. Nor am I game to say anything about Uncle Bertie's having been – a crossdresser? – a transvestite? – a transsexual? What's the right word? I'm shocked, naturally, by the whole thing. Not that there's anything wrong with men dressing as women, or women as men, and so on. We've got over that sort of thing, haven't we, nowadays? Only it's one thing to be tolerant in theory. Quite another thing to know that such a – a trampish travesty – such a person – was one of the family. Our family. Jolly disconcerting.

Actually, bloody appalling!

The taxi driver, catching sight of a sow wandering over the tarmac, tuts and lets out a toot. The sow looks. She shakes herself. She keeps snuffling stolidly on her way. No, I'm not game yet to tackle the topic of Bertie.

Nor, seemingly, is Guy.

The outskirts of Apia look a little like a township in Canterbury. Bungalows hunched down in green gardens. Yet slapdash, shabby. Hot, too. The cab swings around a corner and a big white ziggurat looms up. Odd. Have we taken a wrong turn to biblical Babylon? Or perhaps fascist Italy? The ziggurat proves to be a Mormon temple. We pass more slovenly bungalows. And now we're in the middle of the town, which turns out to be shops of one or two storeys and two or three office blocks of six or seven storeys. We come to a sort of seaside boulevard. Spiky palm trees. Dark people draped loosely with yellow, orange, green, purple, pink. At first glance, the scene seems exotic, certifiably blissful. At second glance, it looks more like a tropical slum.

'Interesting little city, isn't it, darling?' says Guy, being sensible, being good. 'Lots to observe and think about.'

'I don't want to think. I want to drink.'

'I should stop thinking myself. I should try to start feeling.'

A funny thing for him to say. Not at all like Guy. I twist sideways to look at him properly. Nothing out of the ordinary in his wan blue eyes, nothing more than his workaday look, a bit stiff and straight but quiet, tidy.

'We'll be right once we get ourselves a comfy bivouac, Guysie.'

Our driver turns into a driveway. Queen Lupe's Hotel looks more or less consoling. A biggish newish hotel. White clean walls. Shiny glass. Polished brass. A hotel much like any adequate if hardly wonderful hotel anywhere in the world.

Guy, catching sight of the glass, the brass, relaxes palpably.

After a bit, in the end, I relax too.

At the same time I feel faintly let down by the hotel, I'm somehow disheartened by its smooth ordinariness.

Reception offers us what sound like two perfectly decent suites, and two perfectly nice young men carry our bags. I go into my suite. Yes, decent. The main room opens onto a private terrace. I order a gin and tonic. I do some unpacking. I puddle about. I order another gin and tonic. Guy joins me. We talk about the vestry. We talk about Beauchamp. We say nothing about Paradise in Heaven. Night falls as swiftly and suddenly as one knows it's meant to fall in the tropics.

We dine at the hotel restaurant, which proves to be a wide wooden deck laid in tiers around a swimming pool. A pretty young woman shows us to a table. *Sefulu* says her name tag. She wears a red shirt and a long red lavalava and seems shy. A young man brings us drinks. *Fetu* says his name tag. He also wears a red shirt but his lavalava is black and stops at the middle of his very muscled calves. A yellow flower has been tucked behind his left ear and he, too, seems shy. I think I may have mistaken the manners of the young woman at the airport. You know, the lass in the immigration hall. I thought she was being cold. She was most likely just shy.

Or perhaps she was being deferential?

The staff here, perhaps they're being deferential? Young people of modest rank behaving quietly when talking to us because we're older, we're guests, we're – well, chiefs in a way.

Our waiter comes back. A white wine for me, a guava juice for Guy.

'Thank you, Fetu,' says Guy.

The young man grins then looks a bit abashed before loping off, with a powerful springy step, over the wooden deck.

'Nice looking when they're young, aren't they?' I say.

'Who, Pwu?'

'Samoans. The young people are strong but somehow soft.'

'Yes.'

'Fetu isn't just good looking. He's handsome enough to be a male model.'

'Mm?'

The phone begins ringing.

'Hello Mummy,' sings a young woman. 'Safely landed in Tonga?'

'Hello Charley. Samoa. Yes.'

A little stir elsewhere on the deck lets us know that musicians are getting ready to play. Two men, one with his hair twisted into dreadlocks and the other with his hair plaited back in a horsetail. The shirts of both are bright, blooming with tropical flowers. One wears trousers dyed cobalt. The other wears a lavalava of lime green entwined with a design of hibiscus. They hold electric guitars. I know the voices of the men will be good. Samoans are musical, of course.

'Samoa? You *said* Tonga!'

'Did I?'

'You *did* Mummy!'

I didn't.

'Must've been a slip of the tongue, Charley. Anyway, here we are, safe and sound and about to eat dinner. You don't generally get up this early in the morning, do you? Got a shoot today?'

'I've not been to bed yet, Mummy.'

'Is that wise?'

'I'll get some kip in a bit.'

The singing has begun by now. The two men are crooning what seems to be a love song in Samoan. Yes, their voices are good. Charley is chatting in her broken, scrappy sort of way. I look around at other people seated at table. White women and men, mostly. And the bishop from the plane, still in his black lavalava, still gripping his carved stick. He's silent, scowling. No sign of the young fellow in trackpants who was lugging his bags.

'Anything of vital importance going on with our sprog?' asks Guy after I farewell Charley.

'Nothing. I think she was just making sure we're safe and sound.'

'One wonders why she should bother, given that safety and soundness are our hallmark.'

'Well they're not our hallmark now, darling! That's why we're here, aren't we? It's all novelty and adventure for us now! Apropos of which – you know, apropos of novelty and adventure and so on and so forth – '

I stop to sip my wine.

'Apropos – ?' he hints helpfully.

'Apropos – well, sweetheart, how are you feeling about – you know? About – well, about Paradise in Heaven? And about – quite frankly, about Bertie?'

'I take it you mean how am I feeling about the fact that the only uncle I ever loved appears to have ended up living as a woman? And perhaps you also mean how am I feeling about that fact that conceivably, if that image over his grave means anything, he was the lover of the angry man who came out of the dunny?'

'Quite. How are you feeling?'

'Well it takes all sorts, doesn't it? The family always did say he'd gone troppo.'

'You're taking it calmly.'

'Calmly? Ah. How else can one take it, Pwu?'

Guy needs my backing. Not that the poor boy knows how the least hint about Bertie's doings – the lipstick, the yellow hibiscus, the beehive hairdo dyed so deeply – how the faintest whispered word of such things would be wonderful grist to our neighbourhood gossip mill, would be whisked up in a trice by the snapping teeth of tattlers. Whisked up,

93

threshed and then sprayed mirthfully all over the district.

A godsend to Buffy.

'That's the spirit, Guysie. Do you think others in the family might know how – well, quite how *wholeheartedly* he went troppo?'

'Heaven knows.'

'Paradise in Heaven knows,' I say, doing my very best to laugh, or at least to seem to be laughing. 'Anyway, let's get the muddle sorted out with the lawyer tomorrow and then have our holiday – have our holiday come hell or high water – go to some resort or something!'

'Yes, that sounds sensible.'

'Oh, then maybe we shouldn't? If it sounds sensible? I mean, you know – adventure and novelty!'

'I didn't mean sensible. I meant a good way to have – er, fun.'

'Yes! It's what you said before. Feeling, not thinking.'

We eat fish, which is fresh and delicious but sauced too crudely. We chat about this and that. We look up at the palms as they sway. We order coffee. The coffee comes and isn't good.

'Fancy a stroll?' says Guy, setting down his cup. 'The sea wall on the other side of the road looks pleasant.'

'Does it, darling?'

'I scouted the ground soon after doing my unpacking. A good fresh breeze off the water. Vista seawards right out to the reef, landwards up to the main range.'

We sign for our meal, wander down the driveway and cross the road to the sea wall. Yes, the breeze is lovely. The sea wall has been built from hunks of lava and chunks of concrete stepped in a way not wholly unlike the Mormon ziggurat. Steps are tangled in spots with some sort of bindweed. The bindweed leaves are glossy under lamplight. Waves cluck against the base of the rocks. Litter bobs in the waves. Plastic bottles, aluminium cans, nylon cording.

I look one way. I look the other way.

'Jesus is the King of Samoa,' say big white words painted on a corrugated iron roof. 'Samoa is founded on God.'

'I'd rather nest for this evening, Guysie. And anyway it's dark, so no vista. But why don't you go for that stroll by yourself?'

'Right you are. I'll take the phone in case I go astray.'

'Good thinking, sweetheart.'

Off he strolls, while I wander back to my suite and think for a while about Bertie and Paradise in Heaven. I don't know what it might mean, this business of Bertie dressing as a woman and camping on that nasty little scrap of land. How could he be willing to live in that shack? Why did he sink himself into such – well, not to put too fine a point on it – such poverty? Was it that he was wanting to live simply? Was he really poor, or did he choose to live as though he was poor?

The estate hasn't been probated yet. Perhaps his money is salted away?

Or perhaps he lost it? The money. Clearly he lost his mind.

Well, I'll not speculate pointlessly until we can learn more, inform ourselves more fully – the lawyer tomorrow –

I feel too restless to stay in my suite so go down to the restaurant again and sit by the pool and order a glass of the local beer, which proves perfectly drinkable. A type of German lager. Germany owned these islands before we took them over in the First World War. So here's me, sitting, drinking, thinking. My neck aches. The wound on my forehead is throbbing. Why does it always seem that my life is not here, not now, but waiting for me tomorrow? Waiting at the end of a wide empty pathway like that wide empty pathway on top of the sea wall, concrete poured and set on top of cooled lumps of lava. Our goal nearly always seems to be to go, doesn't it? To go, not to be. I'm doing my best to be here, to be here and now, but my eye, my mind, looks beyond here and now to the next step, the next setting. We think that our real lives – if we really do have real lives – our real lives are not here, not now, but tomorrow.

Or – and this is worse – not tomorrow but yesterday.

'*Guy*!' I squeal. 'What have you *done*?'

The poor boy has loomed up suddenly. A lustrous bud of blood swells on the lobe of his left ear and another blooms on the bony ridge of his left cheek. His shirt and trousers are torn and dusty. He looks not like himself, somehow.

He seems to be someone I somehow don't quite know.

Which of course is silly.

'No need to worry, Pwu,' he says, smiling – but a bit shakily. 'I was unwise enough to walk across a park in the dark and some young thug put his foot out to trip me up.'

I jump from my seat to do a quick check of those buds of blood.

'Oh, sweetheart! Anything other than grazes to the head?'

'Nothing worth mentioning. While I was down he did go through my pockets.'

'You poor *darling*! Hold still and let me get a good look at you. Oh dear, quite a few contusions. And look at your clothes, too! Hang on, don't jib. Let me get a thoroughly good look. Well, nothing so very bad. The graze on your cheek is the worst but you won't be needing stitches. We'd better get you to my room straight away and clean you up. It's a good thing I brought my handy little first aid kit. Gosh, we *have* been in the wars, haven't we? Come on, darling. Chop chop!'

The bright white light of my bathroom seems clarifying, purifying. I work swiftly. I work deftly. Mother hen is always a safe role to play. After patting the abrasions with sterile gauze, I pronounce him in no need even of bandages.

'Right you are, Pwu. What shall we do about the phone? The boy took it.'

'Anything else, darling?'

'A few dollars.'

'Not so bad then, is it? We can pop into the police station tomorrow and report the assault and the theft.'

'I won't bother the police by filing a complaint. The boy's more victim than criminal. He's a youngster like that little hoyden who threw the stone at you. As you said yourself, it's just kids, really. The one who attacked me must just be a lad who's lost his way. We can buy a new phone tomorrow.'

'Mm, but then we'd need to phone home, get someone to get hold of our address list, which would be tiresome.'

'It would.'

'We needn't do anything about the phone in a hurry, need we?'

'I don't know. Need we?'

'We needn't, I think. Actually it's quite a relief to have lost the phone. Why don't we have a holiday from being phoned and from phoning? After all, we're meant to be taking it easy.'

'You don't think – ? In case Tim – ?'

'Or Charley – '

Slowly we look each other in the eye. Quite slowly, quite candidly. I think we're having the same thought. I know we're having the same thought. We want a holiday not just from the phone but from Tim and Charley. And, needless to say, after knowledge comes guilt. A mother and father shouldn't think this way.

'Getting hold of the address list would be quite a job, wouldn't it, Pru?'

'It would, Guy. Is it awful of us not to want to?'

'Why don't we just put it off for a day?'

I feel perky, suddenly.

'Yes, let's put it off – perhaps for two or three days?'

'Right you are, Pwu.'

We sit together on my terrace. We talk in a companionable way. I nip back inside, after a bit, to get hold of my hairbrush. Seating myself back on the terrace, I begin brushing my hair the way I do every evening. One hundred strokes with my lovely old brush. Sterling silver, engraved with the Tancred coat of arms, passed down for generations in our family. I have the brush newly tufted every several years. I peer across at Guy. The blood on his cheek and ear lobe is drying. The blood on my forehead has hardened into a good clean scab.

I start giggling.

Guy looks at me wonderingly.

'Look at us!' I say, after some more giggling.

'What about us?' he says, looking at me even more wonderingly.

I burst into loud, choking laughter and point at his cheek and ear lobe, and up at my forehead.

'Score for the first two rounds!' I say with a little yelp. 'Samoa two. Canterbury nil!'

CHAPTER SEVEN

The walls, floor and ceiling of my hotel room look so bland that I find it hard even to think about going outside into the sultry morning. The floor is shiny with tiles the colour of ivory. The walls are painted beige. The ceiling is plastered white. The drapes are thick, the colour of sand. A low hum tells me the room is being kept cool by air conditioning.

'Get a grip, Pru,' I whisper to myself.

You can't spend the whole day inside, hiding, can you?

I grab hold of a drawcord and work it with my right hand. Drapes slide away from glass to show my terrace. Two cane steamer chairs and a cane table. A lawn unrolling beyond the terrace before coming to a stop at a tennis court. A low shrub or two strewing the choppy grass with floppy red flowers. Squinting, looking more closely, I see that the shrubs are hibiscus. At the heart of each red flower is a flare of yellow. The bushes are pretty enough, I suppose, though somewhat shapeless. I can't see any sign of a landscape architect having laid out the grounds. Shrubs are simply plonked about randomly.

I think longingly of Beauchamp.

Beauchamp, where everything has a reason why. Beauchamp, where beyond our orderly grounds we can glimpse our orderly woodlands and our orderly paddocks, all in their neat geometry, and again beyond them the plains cut scrupulously into triangles and squares and oblongs.

Stepping out onto the terrace, I breathe in the heat and – straightaway – start sweating.

Deep breaths, just breathe deeply.

The fragrances are certainly wonderful. Sweet, velvety. Layer upon layer of fragrance. Yes, keep calm, Pru. All's well, isn't it? You're free, healthy. You've nothing to worry about in the world. You're wearing a nice little linen frock. The waist and bodice have been cut to be fitting. The skirt has been cut to be a little full, to hide flaws.

And there's nobody here in Samoa to see – just Samoans.

Two of whom now loom up on my left and walk across the lawn slowly yet purposefully. Workmen, in overalls. One young, one not so young. Workmen doing what workmen do, getting on with the task of tinkering with things that need to be tinkered with, setting things to rights. The not so young one holds an aluminium ladder that winks in the sunlight. The young one, stopping by one of the shrubs, stoops to pick up a blossom and sniffs. His pose, his hold on the blossom, seems somehow – well, dainty.

Oops. He's caught sight of me looking.

He smiles. A nice smile, showing his teeth, which seem very white, though no doubt only by contrast with his dark skin. I smile back. The older workman has walked off to the right. The young man widens his smile, showing more of those big white teeth, and veers towards my terrace, clearly intending to say something.

God, what have I done?

I clutch my terrace railing, which gives me the advantage of feeling that I'm on my own ground.

'Hullo,' he says, in rather a nice baritone. 'What you doing?'

A bit thrown by his directness, I take half a step back, while keeping my grip firm on the railing.

'Oh, hello,' I say politely and, I hope, firmly. 'Just getting a breath of air.'

'You here with your husband?'

What on earth does the man want? Surely he can't imagine it's part of his job to strike up casual conversations with guests who chance to meet his eye. Yet perhaps he does, given that this is Samoa. Who knows what passes for correct behaviour in these islands?

'Yes,' I say, less politely and, I hope, still more firmly.

'Nice,' he goes on. 'Husband not here now?'

Clearly this must be knocked on the head. At the same time he means well, one supposes, so no need to be curt.

'Next door, I imagine. It must be hot for you, working in this weather.'

He surveys me from top to toe, swiftly, in a way that throws me still more than I was thrown only moments ago because it seems – suddenly – something else, something like what happened – or perhaps happened, though who knows? – with that chap, that journalist in the tight black jeans, who came the other month to Beauchamp. I blush at the memory. That chap's very nice bum squeezed into those tight jeans, and his crotch squeezed into the jeans, too. My eyes at one point just went straight down to his crotch and I think –

I can feel myself blushing even more, now!

I looked, and I think he saw me looking, so of course what did I do, silly me? I trotted to the fence of the hack paddock! I did my best to put on a show of getting soppy over Bob, my dear old chestnut, and poor innocent Bob took my caresses at face value, thinking I was having a little fit of fondness for him, and – well, of course I love Bob and of course he loves me, but still –

Surely this young man here on the lawn right now – ? Surely he's not meaning – ?

'You need help, lady?'

'Help?'

His eyes are fixed on mine now. Big eyes. Brown eyes. The black lashes are very long. I'd kill for such lashes. Letting go my grip on the railing, I step back towards the glass door and its smooth safety. He can't be meaning – ? I mean, for heaven's sake, he's handsome, he's young. I'm nearly old enough to be a grandmother! Certainly old enough to be this boy's mother – or pudgy old aunt. I must not be reading things right, clearly.

'I help you, lady?'

'No, no thank you – nothing. Thank you!'

I bolt back through the open doorway. I slide shut the glass. I find myself no longer alone. Guy stands in the middle of the room, smiling. He's wearing a cotton polo shirt and twill slacks. Slacks and shirt the same sandy colour as the drapes. The shirt tucked into the trousers. The trousers cinched in turn with a brown leather belt bought twenty years ago in Ballantynes.

'What was that young fellow saying, Pwu?'

'Oh, nothing – asked me whether I needed a hand. Bit odd, really! Still, when in Rome – '

'If only we were in Rome, darling.'

'Quite!'

After breakfast by the pool we get a taxi which takes us into a warren of hot, weltering side streets. Concrete shops hunker under rusting roofs. The pavements are smeared with oil and petrol. Dark people walking, talking, milling, sauntering, shuffling, plopping about on broad brown jandalled feet, moving slowly. The lawyer's rooms turn out to be inside a wooden house whose weatherboards have been blistered badly by sun and years. Greenery entangles the house on every side while we pick our way forward over a path of flat lava rock. The front door creaks open. We find a young woman, slim and pretty, a flower tucked behind an ear, who looks up at us smilingly.

'Talofa,' she says.

'Talofa,' says Guy, very carefully. 'I'd like to have a chat with Mr Wanderer.'

'Wolfgang?' says the young woman, smiling more broadly.

'Wolfgang Wanderer, yes,' answers Guy. 'I phoned him once or twice yesterday but got no reply.'

'Yesterday he take the day off and send me home too. He take lots of days off. He's here today.'

She waves towards an open inner door. The frame of the door seems quite markedly off plumb. My guess is that the door itself is never closed, given how it hangs so askew. Guy and I step through the doorway. A scrawny old man is seated at a good but nicked teak desk. We see him from the side. The shape of his bent body at the desk is like an upside-down question mark.

'Manuia le taeao,' he says, though he keeps his head down, working his way through a heap of not-quite-white bond.

'Good morning,' we say.

'Please take a seat,' he adds, still without looking up.

We lower ourselves gingerly onto an old wooden sofa whose rattan seat lets out a worried squealing. A wall of law books climbs towards the ceiling. Corners are cobwebby. The lawyer's white hair is bound with a red and purple headband. A raw silk shirt flops from his meagre torso. A cotton lavalava hangs on his shankless lower body. His skin looks leathery.

How many years of sunbathing have baked him that shining reddish brown?

At last, after scratching a few last words on one of the sheets of bond, he throws down his pen and swivels to look at us with watery eyes. He tells us he knows what happened yesterday at Paradise in Heaven. He apologises for not warning us about the angry man with the cropped skull. He goes on to say that paperwork for the estate is straightforward – that no court, here or back home or anywhere else in the world, could do anything upon looking at that paperwork other than allow Guy full right to ownership of Paradise in Heaven.

'Bertie, ven she drew up her last vill and testament after she vas buying that little property,' he says, 'vanted it to be a gift to you, Mr Blandwood – may I have the honour to call you Guy?'

She? Oh for heaven's sake!

'Certainly,' says Guy, stiffening.

We fidget on top of the scratchy rattan while the old man breathes a bit asthmatically.

'And you must call me Volfgang. One can be very clear about the point, as a matter of law. One can also be clear about another point, as a matter of feeling. Bertie, a year or so ago, told me she vanted to change the vill. She had made up her mind not to leave the land to Guy. A month went by. The vill was not changed. The months kept going by. Bertie died. The vill had not been changed. A case of fa'a Samoa.'

Guy looks hurt, fleetingly, but then of course bucks himself up.

'In other words,' he says, 'it's not ethically mine?'

'Ve can say it's legally yours, Guy.'

'Yet not ethically. What did he intend to do with the property, if it wasn't to go to me? Did he want it to go to a charity?'

'Not to a charity as such, but rather to the poor – in a manner of speaking.'

'The poor? Was he no more specific?'

'She vas very specific. She vanted the whole of her estate to go to one poor person, namely her husband.'

Guy gapes.

'His – her – *husband*?'

'Quite so, to Stevenson Tagaloalagi Bismarck.'

'A man can marry a man in Samoa? Surely not!'

'Missy Bertie in her own eyes vas married to Stevenson. Stevenson in his own eyes vas married to Missy Bertie. All of Samoa knew.'

'Missy Bertie?'

'Samoa calls her Missy Bertie.'

'Did anybody in my family – know?'

The answer, we find out, is that the lawyer has no idea and is not very interested in the topic. He goes on to talk about his own story. Although born in Berlin he was the grandson of a couple who had a coconut plantation here when it was a German colony. The grandfather was interned by our army when we took over the colony.

'An internment,' he adds drily, 'qvite against international law.'

'International law was never my field,' says Guy.

'Chinese plantation vorkers vere bayoneted by your army, too, vich perhaps was vithin the law in your country,' he says with no special stress. 'All plantations owned by German citizens vere seized by your government and then the planters vere driven out of the colony. My grandparents vent back to Berlin. Alvays, until their deaths, they told varm loving stories about Samoa and sowed in my imagination the seed that led me to come here myself some tventy years ago.'

I've had enough of this maundering.

'Darling, the land's yours by law,' I point out. 'I think it most likely that Bertie really wasn't sure about whether or not to leave it to – to Mr Bismarck – and made up his mind not to tamper with the will.'

'Only do we really want that rather scurfy scrap of land, darling?'

'Well, probably not – but it must be worth something. We can put it on the market, have our holiday here – you know, stay in a resort – then go home to Beauchamp.'

'Darling,' tries my old boy, 'I think by rights it belongs to Mr Bismarck.'

'No need to be quixotic, sweetheart. We know you're not the best when it comes to handling money.'

Guy looks at me gravely.

'Admittedly money and I seldom seem to understand one another well, but does that warrant robbing Mr Bismarck?'

My turn to feel a little hurt, now.

'Robbery! Well, that's a – strong – word, darling. Mr Bismarck won't go homeless. He'll have ownership rights to communal land elsewhere in the islands, won't he? You know – shared rights? Bertie owned the land. He bought it fair and square. He paid for it with Blandwood money, made from family land in Canterbury. I do think it's only right that the money should come back to Canterbury.'

The lawyer looks at us in an almost fatherly way.

'Vy not try doing things slow, my friends. Let your thoughts drift. See how you feel after a vile. I suggest you both go avay to one of the beaches for a fortnight. No need to hurry. Never any need to hurry, here in Samoa.'

Guy breathes out, very slowly.

'I think you're right, Wolfgang,' he says.

Certainly nothing is to be lost by waiting two weeks, so I agree with a good show of grace. Perhaps the best thing to do really is to make the most of things and try to turn the very hairy and smelly sow's ear of Samoa into – not a silk purse, but at least a set of anecdotes – yarns with which we'll be able to amuse friends and family when we get safely back to Canterbury. We make an appointment to come back to the lawyer's office in a fortnight.

'Can we count on you to be here, behind your desk, a fortnight from now?' I say with a smile but not wholly teasing. 'Are you sure you won't decide to take that day off?'

He giggles.

Guy and I get another taxi and go to the tourist office in the town centre where we look at pamphlets and talk to staff. Two or three beach resorts look more or less luxurious but a bit lacking in – in what? I think it's that they look like the sort of place one would find anywhere from the Algarve to Rio. Almost all other resorts in the pamphlets seem to be pretty simple spots. I quite like the thought of choosing one of the simple spots. So long as the simple spots aren't too simple.

'Teuila Villas look quite nice, darling,' I say.

'Mmmm? Where are they?'

'On the north coast of Savai'i. We'd need to get a ferry. A pretty beach and lagoon and a row of little cottages right on the verge of the sand. The cottages each have their own bathroom and lav, and they each have their own veranda, too. We could sit on our little verandas and watch the lagoon lapping.'

'Very poetic, Pwu.'

'I'm only good enough for prose, Guysie.'

We book two of the cottages. We book a taxi to the ferry. We step out into the heat of the street. A man about our own age, some sort of vendor, greets us smilingly. A worn man with a round belly.

'Hello, sir,' he says. 'Talofa, lady.'

Guy and I voice one or two civil words.

'You wanting helping kindergarten? Buy lovely lavalava for the lady? Money for kindergarten?'

Guy looks about to wave the man away.

'A kindergarten's a good cause,' I cut in. 'What colours do you have?'

'Beautiful colours!'

He pulls a length of cloth from a bag. Violet, printed with a pattern of flowers in lime green, coarse but pretty.

'Oh!' I say. 'How sweet!'

'This one,' says the vendor. 'Good for you, lady.'

'Not necessarily optimal quality, darling,' says Guy.

'It's just a bit of fun, Guysie. I want it!'

I buy. I pay. We climb into another taxi and make our way back to Queen Lupe's. We sit by the swimming pool where a smiling though clumsy waiter takes our orders for lunch. A steak with salad for me. A fruit platter for Guy. The fruit platter proves to be a wise choice. My salad is iceberg lettuce, tossed with a few shreds of cucumber and tomato, swimming in a mayonnaise straight from a bottle. A cheap bottle, too. My steak – well!

Guy swats a mosquito.

'Must toddle to a pharmacy after eating,' he says. 'Get some insect repellent.'

'Perhaps you could also pop into a drapery and pick up a pair of dressmaking scissors? They might help me slice my way through the next steak I order in Samoa. On second thought, perhaps if a hardware shop catches your eye you could make it a pair of secateurs?'

'Is it really so terribly chewy, darling?'

'So chewy one could use it to replace that dreadful old belt you're wearing, sweetheart.'

'Well, as my grandmother used to say, worse things happen at sea, which is why – '

' – she chose to fly,' I chip in, finishing a story I've heard a hundred times over the last quarter of a century. 'Yes, Guysie.'

He looks hurt, once more, but then of course bucks himself up. I feel guilty for snapping. Really, though, he does annoy me now and then when he parrots the same old words over and over again. Not that I'm so scintillating myself! I suppose it's just that when you've been married for so many years you've heard everything the other has to say.

Only, has anyone anywhere anything to say?

I feel a bit flat, suddenly.

Oh dear – why? I mean to say – here I am, seated by a swimming pool under palm trees on a tropical island and really it's rather nice, isn't it? Other than the steak. And the salad. Guy's a good man. Guy's a lovely man. Only – boring – and – and what the hell did that young workman mean this morning when he asked me whether I needed help? I ask you! He's the one who needs help, poor chap, stuck in drudgery. Anyway, life's a lark. The world's low comedy, isn't it, not high tragedy?

I'll wear the lavalava – the lime and violet lavalava – I'll wear it tomorrow.

CHAPTER EIGHT

The *Lady Samoa*, a proper ship, looks serious enough as it strains on hawsers outside its terminal. The terminal, mind you, is not quite what we were anticipating. A low concrete shed under a roof of galvanized steel, it squats next to a tarmac car park. Guy and I look at one another with dismay.

'At first glance a restaurant seems less than likely,' I try, 'but there's bound at least to be a coffee shop.'

'Bound to be,' he agrees hopefully.

The cabbie hefts our bags out of the boot and we follow him into the shed. A concrete floor. A concrete ceiling. Walls and ceiling have been painted a weary white. Open spaces, punched into the walls, let in air from the outside. The outside air is hot. Wooden benches have been screwed onto stumpy steel legs. A big crowd of brown forbearing people sprawls on the seats or ambles about aimlessly.

No coffee shop. Nothing.

'We might have been wise to breakfast at Queen Lupe's after all, Guysie.'

'Oh well. All part of the adventure!'

We sit on one of the benches, not quite knowing why.

'Whew – the air in here!' I say. 'What's the right adjective?'

'Sticky?' says Guy. 'Stifling?'

'Samoan!' I say with a laugh.

A closer look at the crowd shows us soon enough that a handful of other white people are also in the shed. A group of lithe young men and women with backpacks whose tanned thighs shoot sportily out of short shorts are speaking German. A couple of older women dressed in cotton – women who look pretty much at ease – talk together in English. Otherwise, the whole crowd really is Samoan. A lot of them sit crosslegged, their big brown horny feet bare or poking out from cheap jandals. A few are trying to stir the air by waving palm leaf fans which I see have been woven by hand, simply but tidily.

'The ferry's due to sail shortly but nobody seems to be moving,' I say. 'I wonder when we're meant to get on board.'

'I spotted a loudspeaker over there,' says Guy. 'We probably wait for an announcement.'

The loudspeaker is bolted to a concrete pillar.

'Assuming it's wired up,' I say.

'Assuming,' says Guy.

'Peckish?'

'I can cope a little longer, darling. We'll eat on the ferry.'

'I'm awfully thirsty. Gasping for a coffee or a cup of tea. Someone somewhere must be selling. You sit with the bags and I'll take a scout.'

'Right you are, Pwu.'

Gamely, I set off, trying to work my compact little body through the crowd in a way that looks quiet but commanding. A handbag hangs from my edgy shoulder. I'm wearing the lavalava. I've become fond of it already. So vividly lime and violet! Although when I tried getting it on after showering

114

this morning it proved quite tricky to knot the hank of fabric tightly around my less than hourglass waist. Anyway, here we are! Scavenging for refreshments inside this smothering shed in the tropics is not quite me in my element on the open plains of Canterbury but there's bound to be a cup of something for sale and if not inside the shed then outside, through that opening.

As indeed there is, I soon find. A little wooden hutch where a vast brown woman has set up shop.

'Talofa,' I say. 'Tea?'

'Talofa,' she says. 'Sure – how many?'

The tea turns out to be boiling water poured into two white polystyrene cups into which the woman drops two teabags. Well, tea is tea. Gripping a slippery cup in each hand, stepping warily back into the shed – hoping not to be jostled, which might spill some of the tea – I work my way through gaps in the throng.

'Tea!' I sing out when five paces away from Guy. 'We're roughing it, though – Choysa!'

I lift up one of the polystyrene cups as a sort of salute to my prowess at scavenging. The awkward move proves a mistake. The knot in my lavalava unties smoothly. The lavalava unfolds calmly. The whole lot drops to my feet, showing the inmates of the shed my roly-poly hips clad in a pair of what suddenly seem to be startlingly white knickers.

I stop dead.

'Guy!' I squeak. 'Do something!'

The eyes of everyone – children, women, men – turn towards me as I stand stock still, gripping the polystyrene cups. My first thought is that I should throw down the cups, grab the lavalava and tug it up. My second thought is that of course I can't throw down the cups because a child or baby might get scalded with the hot drinks. Guy evidently makes up his mind that the best thing for him to do is simply to look calm and cool, as though it's a common thing for a matronly white woman in the midst of an unknown brown crowd to expose her legs and knickers.

Stooping gingerly, I set down the cups. I hoist up the lavalava. I tie a knot. The eyes are no longer looking my way. Nobody has so much as smiled, let alone sniggered or pointed.

Flushed, sweaty, I stumble forward once more with the two cups.

'Why didn't you do anything?' I hiss to Guy.

'I thought it best to – '

'Honestly, you're bloody hopeless,' I cut in before sitting smartly on the bench. 'You're always in your head.'

'Sorry, darling.'

'So bloody embarrassing, Guy.'

A man seated opposite, an elderly man whose lavalava is also violet, has been observing. He bends forward, now.

'Sorry for you, lady,' he whispers.

Startled, I look up at the man but he turns his eyes away.

'Oh!' I say. 'That's very kind!'

The old man has heard my thanks – he shows it by faintly nodding – but he keeps his eyes turned away. I'm impressed by such collected courtesy. Actually, now I think about it, the manners of everyone else are impressive, too. Although nearly every eye on every side did look at the sight – well, who wouldn't look at a free clown show! – they then looked away, and peacefully, without any signs to one another that something funny was happening, indeed without any sort of stirring.

We sit, sipping our nasty tea.

The loudspeaker bolted to a concrete pillar stays silent. Groups of people, however, begin shuffling towards the ship.

'Loudspeaker not wired up,' I say.

'No,' says Guy.

'Samoa,' I say.

'Samoa,' he says.

We manhandle our bags out to the wharf. No workman offers to help. We manhandle the bags up a ramp. We manhandle them onto a parking deck inside the ship. We manhandle them into a sort of holding pen. We climb a gangway. We know already that the ship has no private cabins and that we must find a space for ourselves on one of two passenger decks. The first deck, enclosed, is crowded and stuffy. No restaurant. No coffee shop. Teabag tea and instant coffee sold in a corner, together with fizzy drinks.

Wordlessly, we climb another gangway.

An open deck, not so crowded. Yellow vinyl seats bolted in rows under a blue awning. Samoan teenagers, laughing. We choose a couple of the vinyl seats in a spot where we'll be shaded when the ship leaves the wharf. The two white women we saw inside the shed – the two oldish women – are seated in the next row, smiling at the world. One of them catches my eye.

'We're not in Kansas anymore,' she says, with a sort of chuckle. 'Are we Toto?'

What? Has the woman been drinking?

'No I suppose we're not,' I try. 'Though I don't quite – ?'

The woman is square. Very square. Packed tight like a little bale of wool. On top, ginger hair cropped short. A cheap dye job. I wonder whether she did it herself. On her lap she holds a backpack. The backpack is nylon – chartreuse with orange piping – and she holds it firmly.

'Not a lover of old Hollywood, then?' she says, giving me a shrewd look. 'What I mean is we're a long way from home. I'm from Auckland. My sister here, too. How about yous two?'

'Canterbury.'

'Name's Lynne, merry widow,' she plunges on. 'Sandy, on my right and a third my biomass, is a gay divorcee.'

Sandy, bony and lightweight, jerks sideways to peer and then wave around Lynne's big bust. The curly hair – a mop of azure blue – on top of her happy head is another cheap dye job.

'That your hubby next to you?' asks Lynne.

'Er, yes. He's Guy. I'm Pru.'

'Cool. I'm a pay clerk. Sandy's admin, which if we're being politically incorrect means receptionist. What do you two do for a crust down in Canterbury?'

'Well, we've got a bit of land.'

'Farming?'

'Not really. We run a few head of stock. We go in for a bit of breeding. We're not very good at it. Here on holiday?'

'Nope! Filial piety.'

'Really? Your parents live in Savai'i?'

'Our mum comes from the island. Our grandparents were schoolteachers in a government school when New Zealand was running Samoa. It was like Maori schools in those days. The teachers whacked any of the kids who spoke Samoan. Our grandparents are still in Savai'i. Six foot under. Mum kicked the bucket last year, back home in Auckland. She talked a lot about Savai'i. Sandy and I thought we'd bring her ashes and scatter them over our grandparents' grave.'

She pats what I now see is a boxlike shape inside the chartreuse backpack.

A bit too friendly, but still – the sisters seem quite nice, in a knockabout sort of style, and I'm willing enough to go on chatting. We swap notes about Samoa. We talk about the lack of food on the ferry.

'Frankly,' I say, 'I'd kill right now for poached eggs on toast.'

Lynne grins.

'I'd bloody lay about with a poleaxe for a mince pie!'

Good earthy women and, to a point, good company. The ferry leaves the wharf, swings about and steams west. Children run and play. Young men swing their hips from steel struts. A sea breeze strokes the scab on my forehead. A seabird, having hitched a ride in our slipstream, hovers watchfully above the waves. The waves are a beautiful deep blue – and Savai'i looms, green and indigo.

The ship, after an hour or so, slows its engines and draws towards the wharf at what we know from maps is Saleleloga, the only township on Savai'i. Guy nods at me quickly, meaningfully. Aware of how to read the nod, I spring to my feet, smile at Lynne, smile at Sandy, say how enjoyable it was to chat and wish them well with the ash sprinkling. The two sisters, staying seated while waiting for others to clear the deck, wave farewell vigorously.

'Gosh,' I whisper, bumping against Guy as we head towards the gangway. 'Decent women but it was a bit of an effort.'

'You handled them beautifully.'

We get our bags, walk down a ramp. Saleleloga turns out to be a straggle of shops and churches and a few bungalows. Our resort is half an hour away. We take pains to find a taxi with air conditioning.

'I wonder what these beach villa thingies are going to be like,' I say. 'Think they'll be any chop?'

'Not holding my breath.'

'Wise.'

Villages go flying by. Savai'i seems even poorer than Upolu. Almost all the houses are no more than thatch or iron roofs propped on top of wooden posts. A lot of the iron is rusty. Fowls pecking. Pigs snuffling. Dogs snarling. We get, in the end, to a village unlike the others – an orderly village – houses painted yellow and blue. We can see, between lush

jungled spurs, an aquamarine lagoon and the curve of
a soft golden strand.

'Paradise?' asks Guy.

'Heaven,' I reply.

Teuila Villas sit in a row in green grounds bordered
with breadfruit trees and coconut palms. Walls are
clad with slabs of lava. A red flower sprouts all
about, spiky and vivid. Guy tells me that it's a type
of ginger and called teuila and is the national flower
of Samoa. A young man steps onto a veranda and
wanders towards us, smiling broadly, his powerful
thighs stirring a lavalava dyed as many hues as a
rainbow.

A very tall young man – handsome, too, very
handsome – so handsome as to be startling.

'Welcome to Teuila Villas,' he says, big eyes
sparkling. 'My name Tui.'

'We have a bird back home we call tui,' I say.

The young man looks at me in a slightly
bewildered way.

'Two villas have been booked for us,' puts in
Guy. 'Our name is Blandwood.'

'I'm Pru,' I add. 'My husband is Guy.'

'My name Tui, yes,' he says once more, smiling.

The villas, when he shows them to us, prove to
be pleasant. We go first to the villa waiting for Guy.
A bedroom, a bathroom and a living room. Simple
and clean, with good plumbing. A veranda
overlooking the lagoon. Guy begins breathing more
easily. Tui takes me next door to my own villa, a twin
of Guy's. The young man seems so pleased with my

obvious pleasure in the place that after unlocking the doors and throwing open a window or two he seats himself on a sofa and flexes the toes poking out from the tips of his orange jandals.

'Comfortable?' I say ironically.

'Yes, fank you, Pru.'

I step backwards and forwards, settling my things onto shelves and into cupboards, and talk to Tui. Or rather, out of idle curiosity, I get him to talk. He tells me he comes from a family of one son and several daughters, adding that while there was enough money to send him to the University of the South Pacific the family has to keep a close eye on spending and makes most of its living by working the tribal land.

'You eat what you grow?' I ask. 'Or sell on the market?'

'We make the plantation to grow our own crops, for family consumptions. My dad want me to study at university. Yes. He don't want me to do any chores or something like that. He passed away.'

'Sorry to hear that, Tui.'

'I study only one year at uni. Too hard. Too lonely. Yes. I get job at Teuila Villas. Teuila Villas belong my Aunty Gussy. Aunty Gussy my mum aunt.'

'Your mother's aunt?'

'Yes.'

'Do you live with your mother?'

'My mum stay in another village. I stay in this village with two my sisters and nieces and nephews. My mum is a good person. Yes. She loves us. And she helps us a lot when we are in school. My school fee in the university in the first year – where am I going to get that? I can't! So my mother is so busy at that time, calling her sisters, and her families in Auckland, to get the money. And she always gave me good advices. Yes.'

'Samoa is pretty. Is there anything you don't like here?'

'Nothing. We fank God for his protection, and blessings he gave us, and we also ask for forgiveness and blessings upon us.'

The young man wanders away after a while, allowing me to get on with my nesting. The walls inside my bedroom and living room are hung with lengths of tapa. I like the look of the tapa. The motifs are geometric or from the wild world. Turtle, centipede, fish, crayfish. The colours are cream, amber, cinnamon, chocolate, cocoa.

'Race you to the water!' I sing from my veranda as I step outside in my swimming togs and see Guy standing in his own togs, on his own veranda, looking wonderingly at the lagoon.

'Done!' he cries.

I bound off the veranda excitedly. I leap onto the sand. I scamper towards the lagoon. Guy, pumping his gangly limbs, runs past – keeps running – and has already done a dive while I'm still splashing my way forwards, still marvelling at the wonderful warm weight of the water dragging against my legs.

'Happy you won?' I cry.

'We've both won,' he answers, laughing. 'Nobody can lose in this lagoon!'

I take a quick dive myself, do a few strokes underwater, then pop my head up to the sun and the sky. Guy's nearby, grinning. We swim. We float on our backs. Breakers crack on a coral reef. Palms nod on the foreshore. Seabirds wheel, cry. Gulls. Terns of some sort, with red tailfeathers. Silvery fish flicker below. Guy, flipping over, starts swimming a steady freestyle. I keep floating. Closing my eyes, I do my best to think of nothing, to want nothing, to forget everything, to regret nothing. Good luck with that – my brain keeps swarming with regrets, memories, wishes, thoughts. The lagoon, though – the lagoon is calm, a balm, beauty, bounty.

Afterwards, we sit on my veranda drying out.

'Heaven,' I say over and over again. 'Utter heaven.'

The food at the resort restaurant is not quite so heavenly. We find ourselves gnawing rubbery poultry, nibbling watery salads. Our mood, however, stays buoyant. The young women who wait at table are very friendly. Our seats at table, on a wooden deck under a big red awning, let us look out at the lagoon. A group of young men can be seen raking the golden sand. A flock of chatty little green parrots, tipped with red flashings, fossick in shrubbery.

After sitting contentedly over coffee – and saying hardly anything for quite a while – we stroll back to our villas.

'Race you to the water!' I yell out again.

'We'll grow gills,' says Guy.

'I feel so good when I'm in the lagoon, don't you darling?'

'I do.'

The afternoon goes by. Our swim we follow with a nap. The nap we follow with another swim. We sit on our verandas, watch the waves, go swimming again, slope down the main street of the village and dine at another resort. The village is very tidy. Sand yards in front of every villa are raked carefully. The villagers meet our eyes and when we smile and speak they smile and speak in reply.

'Talofa,' we say.

'Talofa,' they say. 'Where are you going?'

'A walk,' we say. 'Where are you going?'

'Just going home,' they say. 'Just going work.'

The restaurant at the other resort is no better than the one at ours but we turn a blind eye. We chew. We swallow. We sip a crisp white wine from Otago. We stroll back along the sand to Teuila Villas. The village is on our right. The lagoon is on our left. The lapping of the lagoon is soft, so very soft.

Days go by. I don't think I've ever before stayed anywhere this simple, other than when tramping in the high country in my younger days. Yet it's charming. I love it! The lagoon is lovely. The beach is divine. Cocks crow at all hours, which somehow is calming. Geckoes chirrup while they scuttle – green and supple – up and down the walls. Otherwise, peace! Who'd have thought something so cheap could be so sweet?

All I have to think about is me – oops, and Guy of course!

Bertie's sordid scrap of land with its rocks and heat and rough people could hardly be further away.

Yes, the resort and the village feel like a dreamy picnic spot and as our days go by we really do seem to be permanently picnicking. Admittedly it's a picnic with not very good food and even Guy, who happily would eat wood if someone told him it was bread, finds the menu to be pretty hard going. After asking around we find an adequate restaurant down the beach a bit. We dine there every day. Also we find a little bar run by a young couple from Zurich.

I spend hours splashing in the lagoon – or lolling.

The other guests are something of a motley crew. A correct but reserved elderly couple from Hamburg. A laughing pair of lesbian businesswomen from Wellington. A smug and ignorant group of Mormon missionaries from Utah. A woman and man about sixty years old, rough as sacks, from Sydney. The woman keeps her white hair cropped like a convict and shrugs mottled shoulders out of cheap strappy frocks. She first hoved into view while walking along a path swigging beer from a bottle. Her husband, a big shapeless fellow, wears baggy khaki shorts and a black singlet. How can they manage to find the money to stay at Teuila Villas?

Perhaps they won a lottery.

Guy and I find ourselves seated next to them at breakfast one day. The husband is bolting down fried bacon and eggs. The wife is tucking into what seems a forequarter of pig's weight in fried sausages. Jaws are gnawing. Raw elbows are flexing. I catch the eye of the woman, inadvertently, so do my duty by smiling in what I hope is an amiable way. She widens her own mouth – a very meagre strip of chapped lips – into a rather gruesome grin. Gaps between her front teeth show a shred or two of pork.

'Stinking hot bloody morning!' is her dignified opening.

'Isn't it?' I reply. 'I dare say you'll be down to the lagoon after breakfast?'

'No way. Me mouth's like an Abo's armpit this morning. I'll have a lie down by the pool, just to nurse me hangover.'

I shudder involuntarily.

The woman, I see with alarm, has caught the shudder. Her eyelids narrow, though she says nothing.

Guy seems perky. Very perky. I don't quite know why. He's been taking long walks by himself every evening after dark. And during daylight hours when not rolling about in the lagoon he's lolling on the land, like me – which isn't at all like Guy. He suns himself on the sand. He whistles little songs – though his whistling is flat. Also, interestingly, he seems to have taken a break from reading.

'Sweetheart,' I say, turning away from the Sydneysiders, 'do you know what to call those little green and red parrots?'

'Sega, darling. Sega'ula in some villages. Segavao in other villages.'

'Nice melodious name – looked them up in a book?'

'Asked young Tui.'

Yes, it's like a picnic.

CHAPTER NINE

At the end of our seventh day, yet another balmy night. Anyone who should care to track me down – which nobody does, thank goodness – would be able to find me seated quietly on my veranda. I'm looking out to sea. I'm looking up at the stars. A light trade wind is wafting off the lagoon, whispering promises of ease, promises of peace – promises of all sorts of lovely things.

Guy came back a while ago from his potter down the beach in the darkness and said goodnight. Myself, oddly enough, I'm sleeping less these days. I sit up into the night. Just me on my tod. I nurse a drink. I keep sitting. I keep looking at the stars. Rather mindlessly. Delightfully mindlessly. I keep nursing the drink. I drink less here than back at home. No need to unwind since I'm unwound already! Things that seem so pressing back at home don't matter. Feeling good is what matters. I've stopped wearing makeup. I don't bother with any of my jewellery. I wear the lavalava all day and all night. I've learnt the trick of how to knot it, thanks to one of the nice lasses on the staff. My hair's become a bit of rat's nest – tangles, salt and sand – but who cares?

'Keek keek keek,' says a gecko.

The breeze is lovely.

I notice a movement out of the corner of my eye and see somebody walking along the beach, which arouses my curiosity. Who's out walking at this time? The walker comes closer and, catching sight of me, gives a wave. Tui. I wave back. He approaches, smiling, his feet scuffing the sand.

'Hi, you up late,' he says, stopping at my feet. 'You not sleep?'

'Not yet. Happy the way I am.'

He giggles.

'You happy here?' he asks.

'Very. You're awake late too, aren't you? What have you been up to, Tui?'

He giggles again.

'Just been to see my mum. Yes. She sick.'

'Oh dear. What's wrong?'

'Samoa sickness.'

'Oh? And what's that exactly?'

He shakes his head, shrugs.

'Not good. Sick.'

Other than swapping a few greetings, it's a bit of a strain to talk to the villagers. Only a few speak any more than one or two phrases in English. As for my trying to pick up Samoan – well, it's quite a complicated language. Tui may be a lovely lad but already the conversation is beginning to feel a bit too hard and the best thing would be find some way of winding it up.

Only now he sits down on the steps, obviously settling in for a long chinwag.

Oh.

I notice how, under the moonlight, his face is simply stunning. His shoulders, too – his massive shoulders in a skimpy little tanktop.

'Yes,' he says. 'You happy here?'

'Very,' I say, wondering whether we're going to spend the next hour going round and round and getting nowhere, like two drugged horses on the racecourse at Riccarton.

Only now he floors me completely.

'I make you more happy?'

My opening gambit is to begin tittering.

What on earth does he mean by asking – ? Very likely he wants to know whether he can make me happy by keeping me company in this way. Or does he mean – ? A quick look at his eyes – his moonlit eyes – and I know, suddenly. Golly – didn't spot that coming! Surely I've got it wrong? I think, fleetingly, of that young workman speaking to me at Queen Lupe's – then, even more fleetingly, of that journalist chap at Beauchamp.

Clearly my best strategy is swift withdrawal.

'Well, it's been lovely chatting, Tui,' I say, standing up and speaking in what strikes me as a strangled high voice. 'I'd better get myself off to bed, now.'

He bounds up the veranda steps – comes to a stop.

He puts a hand on my bottom.

I'm shocked.

The intention is very definitely clear. Really? Me? Me being felt up by – by this young god! The last time anyone put his hand on my bottom in a manner even slightly suggestive was – was – heaven knows when – long ago. Too long ago! Guy will rest his palm in the small of my back, now and again, but nobody for years and years has cupped his hand around my bottom. And such a hand! A hand that feels very real, very strong. I stand stock still. I'm reeling.

He kisses my neck.

His lips are soft. I shiver – a shiver going all the way through my body.

'I like you, yes,' he says gently. 'You got a good look.'

I pull away, turn to face him, and frown nervously.

'Oh – ah, thank you, Tui.'

He kisses my lips.

What in christ's name does he think he's – I mean to say, what on earth – ? I don't – I mean, I don't get it. Yet the fingertips of my right hand, not following any overt orders from anywhere near my brain, creep up, slide up, snake their way around his neck. And what a neck! Firm, fabulously firm, flexible, smooth. I gulp, swallowing – nearly choking. His tongue probes between my lips.

I pull away.

I can't do this. This isn't right. This isn't allowed. This sort of thing – you know, a married woman and some strange youth, some young islander – it's just plain wrong. Only he kisses me again, and it feels so nice, and – and, what the hell, why not go along with it for a little. It's been such a long time since I've felt anything like this – this – well, what exactly am I feeling?

A stirring. A yearning down – you know, down there!

Christ, it's been so long since I've felt anything down there. So long, so very long.

I lift my fingertips back up to his neck.

Once more his hand cups my bottom and – slowly – I slide my own spare hand onto his bottom.

Oh! A round, ripe cheek. I want to bend down and bite. He pulls me in more closely. I feel – I feel terrific. I'm kissing him back. Tongues jousting. I always loved kissing. I'm getting hot. So hot! And – and I want to devour, to be devoured – and why the dickens can't I think of words that don't sound like Mills and Boon?

'Come,' he says, taking my hand.

'What? Why – ? Where?'

'Come!' he repeats.

All right, I'll go with him – it's just a kiss or two – it's nothing more – nothing wrong. Holding hands, we walk along the beach till we get to a spot where the moonlight can't find us, a dark spot under a big palm, and he tugs me down onto the sand. I try to sit, to keep some control. Tui pushes me down, right onto my back and then, sprawling on the sand alongside me – his big muscled body – he leans forward and kisses me again, and again, and again. I feel like Deborah Kerr in that old classic film, what's it called? *From Here to Eternity*.

Me, under a palm tree on a tropical beach, getting kissed by a native boy not much more than twenty.

We're not in Kansas anymore, are we Toto?

Golly!

He takes off his tank top. Golly *golly*! He slides a hand up my lavalava. Oh my god! He can't – can he? A hand slipping along my thigh then burrowing inside my knickers. Oh my god oh my god oh my god!

Surely I shouldn't be doing this, but –

Well it's just a bit of foolery, isn't it? No need to get too intense about –

The young workman at Queen Lupe's pops back into my mind. And the journalist chap squeezed into the tight jeans at Beauchamp. I've been living like a nun – a nun in a world where nuns don't have much fun. I'm not a nun. I'm a woman whose blood pumps – or perhaps it doesn't pump so much as trickle, but still –

Two fingers are right inside me, two big blunt fingers, slipping in easily. I'm very wet. He goes on kissing, kissing. The big blunt fingers in and out. I'm not thinking any more about whether I should be doing this, or not doing this. All I'm thinking is oh this is so good, oh how I've been missing for this for so long.

He pulls down my knickers, flicks them onto the sand.

Quick as a wink, his own shorts – tight little rugby shorts – are off. He's on top of me. He's inside me. His face above me, his eyes looking down – hard to see in the dark, only a shiny glitter. Oh he's so beautiful. His chest, his shoulders, his neck, his forehead, his nose, his mouth. All my nerves are lit up. My whole body is alive.

I burst into tears.

Joy, I'm weeping with joy. I never thought I'd feel – feelings. I'm overwhelmed by feelings. It's as though my whole body wants to weep. This is good, so good.

His face tightens up – I can see what's coming.

'Uh, uh, uh,' he says.

'Tui, Tui,' I'm saying.

'Nice,' he says, rolling off me, pulling up the rugby shorts, standing. 'Why you cry?'

All of a sudden I see myself through his eyes. An ageing white woman who's been writhing on the sand, lavalava up around her waist, hair dishevelled, whimpering with bewildered happiness. I'm appalled. He's pulling his tank top over his torso.

'I was crying because I'm silly, Tui.'

'You look pretty,' he says.

'Thank you,' I answer. 'Oh goodness, I shouldn't have done this.'

'Secret,' he says, smiling down at me. 'You and me, secret.'

'A secret? Yes, that's good – mum's the word.'

He looks at me blankly and then, after a bit, sighs heavily.

'My mum so sick,' he says. 'Can't work, can't eat, hurting all the day.'

'You're a good son, Tui, to worry so much about your mum.'

'Fanks, I go now,' he says, standing, pulling me to my feet – not a struggle for a young man so strong.

I feel slightly dismayed by his perfunctory manner. A little more kissing would be nice. Yet perhaps it's wisest, it all happened so quickly and now it's over and I don't know what to make of it. Need I make anything of it? Tropical sands. A moonlit night. Nothing too startling, is it?

'Good night, Tui.'

I walk back slowly, wondering.

The next few days are a puzzle. At the start of each morning I tell myself it won't happen again but by dinner every evening I'm restless. After dinner I start hoping. I pick a flower from a shrub in the resort grounds. A hibiscus. The petals are the same shade as on the shrubs I saw outside my hotel room in Apia. Scarlet. Scarlet and floppily soft. At their heart, a scarlet spike pokes up. A long scarlet spike. A long slippery scarlet spike. The pistil. At its top, yellow anthers. Dustily yellow. Achingly yellow.

Sex.

You think about sex, don't you?

I mean, when you look at a hibiscus flower.

The red petals are you – you down there – and the red pistil is his cock.

I tuck the flower behind my ear, like the girls of the village. After two drinks on my veranda I begin fidgeting. After one or two more drinks I'm anxiously surveying the beach and silently screaming. I no longer put up any pretence of a struggle when he does slope along at last. I no longer wear knickers under my lavalava. I wear a bra that he can unhook easily, though he never does seem to get around to unhooking.

I feel wicked, of course, during the day when I'm with Guy. Also guilty. My poor boy, my poor Guy. He's not looking too perky, now. I don't know why. Odd, given that he was so very perky the first few days here at Teuila Villas. Bertie? The shock of finding out about Bertie – has it begun to take its toll?

'Still having fun, sweetheart?' I try, broaching the subject one afternoon over a gin and tonic. 'You seem a bit – well – under the weather?'

'Do I, darling?' he says vaguely, looking out at the lagoon.

'Mmmm.'

'No no, fit as a fiddle. I imagine I'm just unwinding in my own way.'

'Are you *quite* sure nothing's awry?'

'All perfectly well with my little world, darling.'

So that's that, I dare say. At least I've done my duty by asking.

I feel like – like a piece of fruit – like a breadfruit, a big, ripe, plump breadfruit being plucked nightly. And oh my gosh – the plucking!

After a lovely roll under the palm on the fourteenth night we lie quietly for a bit on the sand. Tui crooks his right arm behind my back. He seems, for once, to be in the mood not to hurry away but to talk.

'I have to educate more, get a better job,' he says. 'I have to work, and care for my parents while they are still alive, and my little sisters.'

'And other than work, what do you want from life, Tui?'

'I want to buy a land in Apia, build a house, buy a car. I need to have a land in Apia to make it easier so I can work. I totally can't save money. I have to do everything my family want. If I had a lot of money I will watch television, go for walk, have a shower, talk on the phone.'

He stops, suddenly.

He stares out at the night sky. The moon is dying.

'What are you thinking about, Tui?'

'My mum. Yes.'

'Oh?'

'My mum worse. So sick.'

'Who's looking after her?'

'Hospital. Yes. No money, and hospital cost a lot. Yes, hospital cost a lot. A lot of tala.'

'How much do you earn a week?'

'Forty tala.'

'Wait here, Tui.'

I jump to my feet. No need to pull up knickers! I scamper across the sand to my villa, snatch my purse, fish out a couple of banknotes, scamper back across the sand. I thrust the notes – two hundred tala – at Tui. He ducks his head, looks down at the sand.

'Fank you,' he mumbles.

'For medicine,' I say briskly. 'For your mother.'

'Fank you. You very kind. Yes. You a very nice lady.'

Am I a nice lady? Here am I giving money to a lover while my husband sleeps innocently only a few stones' throws away. Best not to think about it. This is just a naughty interlude. Never to be repeated. Or at least, never to be repeated once we leave Savai'i.

'You're a nice young man, Tui.'

'We are here to care for our families and live a good life. We are here to help people, help each other. Yes.'

CHAPTER TEN

Guy looks even less perky when we meet over breakfast next morning. Time for me to step in, I think. I suggest that we go on an outing. Guy says nothing. I add that it might be a lark to taxi back to Saleleloga. Guy raises an eyebrow. We need to do some shopping, I point out. He asks what we need to buy. We need to buy a phone, I say, to make good the one stolen in Apia. Also we can have a poke around the market. Quite frankly the last thing I feel like doing is trailing in the heat through some shabby little market in a shabby little township like Saleleloga. Guy needs to be taken out of himself, however, it's pretty plain to see.

'Saleleloga won't have a wide choice of phones, but needs must,' I say. 'We can make do with something cheap for now and perhaps pick up something better when we get back to Apia.'

Chattering away, I talk him around and he gives in with his usual good grace. A cab turns up shortly. We're soon bucketing along the coastal road past banana palms and pigs and coconuts.

'Look at all the great big churches,' I say, still chattering, working at cheering him up. 'How can such poor villages have such showy churches?'

'Tithing. Something we abolished with the Protestant Reformation.'

'Tithing? What's that?'

'A tax levied on the congregations by the clergy.'

'Must be a burden for people who earn so little. Imagine the blank looks if our vicar back home tried tithing!'

Saleleloga, straggling through groves of teeming greenery, proves to have very few shops. The market stinks under a corrugated iron roof and its stallholders sell shirts, eggplant, fans, taro, tapa cloth, tomatoes – but no phones. I plant myself in front of a ragged display of shell beads. I begin picking through one clattering clunky necklace after another, smiling to myself in a way that strikes me as not quite apt for the task in hand. At home, or in Europe, I'd never give more than a passing glance to such tat.

I'm thinking, meanwhile, about Tui.

I pick up one of the necklaces – volutes and cowries strung on some sort of plant fibre – and hold it against my fat little breasts.

'Are you worried about not having a phone, darling?' asks Guy. 'We're rather out of the loop without one, aren't we?'

I turn away from a cracked little glass into which I've been trying to squint and judge the effect of the necklace.

'Actually I rather like being out of the loop – it's very restful. Why don't we give up on looking for a phone? At least while we're here in Savai'i. Can't matter for a few more days. Let's buy one when we get back to Apia.'

He looks at me. I look back at him.

'Fair enough,' he says.

'How deliciously wicked! And I'm going to buy this necklace, just for fun.'

The stallholder can hardly believe her luck when the white customer doesn't bother to haggle but instead pays the asking price. I slip the necklace over my head. The shells bounce about on my breasts. We walk to the end of a row of stalls, turn a corner and see a strikingly goodlooking young man gleaming in the sunlight, his chest and buttocks crammed inside tank top and rugby shorts.

'Oh!' I say.

I can feel myself beaming.

The young man, though, looks at us disconcertedly.

'Hello, Tui!' I cry, far too heartily. 'How lovely to run into you!'

'Good afternoon, yes,' he says, looking down, looking up. 'Where you going?'

He very likely feels awkward seeing me out here in the open, in company with my husband, my betrayed husband.

'We're doing a bit of shopping!' I yelp. 'Seeing the sights of Saleleloga!'

A woman, perhaps about sixty years old, a pink flower in her plaited and oiled hair, steps across from a stall and hands him a bag of breadfruit before stopping by his right elbow and staring at us, not aggressively. She seems to feel she possesses some sort of property rights in Tui.

'This lady my mum,' he says.

'Very nice to meet you, Mrs – er,' I say. 'Good to see you looking so well.'

The mother looks surprised.

'Of course I looking so well!' she says. 'I always so well – so strong lady, me!'

The mother is indeed a fine strapping woman clearly enjoying robust and rude good health.

'You weren't well lately, though?' I try.

The woman looks at me blankly.

'Always so well!'

'Pru,' cuts in Guy, 'we'd best be getting on, don't you think?'

My poor old boy looks sick. The heat, I suppose. The heat under the iron roof. And the smells. And the throng of people. As for me, I want to cry. I haven't cried for years, I understand suddenly. I need to cry. I need to cry and cry and cry.

We say goodbye, steer ourselves away.

'Nothing very interesting to buy here, sweetheart,' I say. 'It's all just ragtag and bobtail and – and so hot, and – nasty. Let's just cut our losses and get a taxi back to the villas. I'm feeling a little seedy. Must be that fish at breakfast.'

'Right you are,' he says flatly.

We get a cab.

Coconuts and pigs and banana palms.

The cabbie is singing a hymn in chorus with his radio when we swing around a bend and run right over a little yellow dog.

'Oh!' I say. 'Stop!'

I shake the cabbie by his shoulder but he's gunning the car rather than slowing. He doesn't care about some stray dog. The skinny dogs in the villages – you see them everywhere, fossicking listlessly for food while ducking stones or curses – are mostly strays.

I start crying.

'I don't think many drivers here would stop for a dog, darling,' says Guy.

'Has he killed the poor thing?'

'No, but he wounded it in the hindquarters.'

'This place is *beastly*!' I say, slumping sideways.

Guy pats my hand. My tears are falling freely. Guy will be wondering why. After all, our families have been docking and gelding and branding and scalping and skinning and flaying dogs and sheep and cattle and horses ever since we took up our land so many generations ago. Why would a crushed cur make me unhappy?

He wraps a bony arm around my flabby little shoulder.

'Not long till we're back at the villas, Pwu,' he says. 'And look over there – those beautiful purple clouds clustering around Silisili.'

'Silly – what? Do you think I'm being silly?'

'Mount Silisili, highest peak on Savai'i.'

'Oh. Yes, pretty. And, well – you know, I really am silly, Guysie.'

We take the last stretch to the villas more calmly and then, when we get there, give ourselves up to swimming and sunning and more swimming. We don't talk a lot. I don't feel a lot. I've had my cry. Tui isn't worth my tears, is he? We agree to skip dinner since neither of u seems hungry. My stomach is in too many knots – too tormented by thinking about that lying young man – to be able to cope with the oily meals of the resort.

'I want nothing more than a cup of tea,' I say.

'Right you are.'

We sit side-by-side on my veranda watching the dusk darken and the tide roll out towards the reef.

'I'm a bit – ,' Guy says at one point in a somewhat subdued voice. 'I'm a bit sick of the villas, Pwu.'

'Oh? Time to pack our traps you think?'

'Only three more days to our appointment with the lawyer in Apia. Toddle back tomorrow?'

'Why not! I'm keen to get a good look at the market in Apia, too. It's so much better stocked than that little tip in Saleleloga.'

I go to bed early and lie on my back while listening to the surf on the reef. I look up at the ceiling, its thatch and timbers, its darkness and deeper darkness. I feel a fool. A gecko somewhere keeps me company.

CHAPTER ELEVEN

Queen Lupe's. The walls and ceiling of my room look so bland, so banal, that the whole horrible thing at Teuila Villas – the thing with Tui – seems far away. Yet still I feel ashamed, and bruised, and angry. The room is the same one I had when we first came to stay. The beige walls. The white ceiling. The floor shiny with ivory tiles. The drapes – still thick, still comforting – still hiding the hot and harassing outside world.

A low hum tells me that the room is still being kept lovely and cool by air conditioning.

We've been here for three days already. I slept nearly eleven hours the first night and since then have kept sleeping. I go early to bed in the evening. I get up late up in the morning. I snooze after lunch. Sleep's lovely, isn't it? You snuggle down. You close your eyes. You're out. You're free from being awake, of having to do this or that – of having to think.

That bloody lying little Tui!

Well, not that he *is* little. Unluckily for me he's a lovely big armful.

Awakening every morning I try to pull myself together, try to laugh it off. But it was so nice. So nice to be kissed, to be – well to be fucked, frankly. Yet all he wanted was my money.

'Now, Pru,' I tell myself, 'don't dwell on what can't be mended.'

I grab hold of the drawcord, which is still good and strong. Once more I work it firmly with my right hand. Once more drapes dyed the colour of sand slide away from shining sheets of glass. Once more a lawn unrolls towards the tennis court. Once more the red blossoms of hibiscus are strewn on the grass. Floppy scarlet petals. Slippery scarlet pistils. A dusting of yellow anthers. I don't step across the lawn to pick up one of the blossoms. The very thought of tucking a blossom behind my ear – of trying to kid myself I'm some village beauty – makes me feel like cringing.

I look about, wondering vaguely whether a workman might wander by. Or, more precisely, the young workman who spoke to me that first day.

No workman wanders by.

'Ready for the day's adventure, darling?' says Guy, after knocking on my door. 'Let's sort out this business of the land.'

We're going to see Wolfgang. After that, we'll drive out to Paradise in Heaven.

I twist my mouth into a smile.

'Yes, sweetheart. And then we can go home!'

The grey old darling looks even greyer lately. He's wearing baggy shorts down to his knees and has tucked a baggy shirt into the waistband. Oh dear. To think that he's my husband. To think that he's supposedly the compass of my passion. Guy Blandwood. A reclusive introvert living in a wishy-washy world of fawn and buff and khaki and – and – I mustn't think this way. I mustn't be a cow. I mean to say, what's he been landed with in *me*? A lumpy, dumpy, short, shallow, vacuous –

I mean, what's special about this ageing woman who's standing in judgement on this ageing man?

Nothing!

That's why I settled for him in the first place, I suppose, and why he settled for me. We weren't game enough to play. We stood watching the polo. We lacked what's wanted to get into the chukka, to whack the ball at the goal. I mean, I thought I was being a bit wild when I knocked around Italy with my sister after finishing varsity but it was quite ordinary really. The right places to stay. The right places to eat. The right places to drink. The offs, on the other hand – well, Charley's always whizzing away to stylish spots, always has some gorgeous man on the go. Tim, too. He lives high in Hong Kong.

A cab takes us through the streets of Apia.

Is it me, or does this town seem worse every time I look at it? How much rust can gnaw into corrugated iron before it falls to bits? How many dogs can scrounge enough from the gutters to keep their mangy bodies and souls not quite together? How many fat shouting young mothers can keep clouting their little kids around the head without making mush inside every skull?

'Getting hot,' says our driver.

'Yes,' I say testily.

Hot – I'm so sick of heat!

Wolfgang proves not to be inside at his teak desk. We have to fight our way outside, dodging rank trunks, stringy creepers and leathery green leaves before finding him splayed in the sun on a crippled deck chair. I haven't seen that sort of deck chair for years. Wooden struts and a saggy canvas seat striped white and yellow. One corner, lacking a leg, has been jacked up onto a pile of mossy bricks. Birds are screaming from treetops. Wolfgang waves vigorously – almost as though waving us away.

'Wilkommen!' he calls out. 'Bienvenus!'

'Talofa,' we say.

He's smiling, baring teeth that seem very long and very yellow. He's stark naked, or nearly. A tiny pair of bikini togs, crimson lycra, cling to the sweaty, oily, ruddy skin stretched over his long, meagre, gangly body. A string of wooden beads hangs from his neck. The beads are a shiny orange. The neck is red and mottled. Sweat, dripping from his head, hangs on coarse white hairs tangled over his scrawny chest.

'How have you got on vith your mulling over?' he asks, standing before taking a lavalava off a bush. 'Vat do you vish with Paradise in Heaven?'

'We don't know,' says Guy.

Wolfgang begins wrapping the lavalava around sharp hips and hollow waist.

'No decisions at all?' he asks, cocking a bushy white eyebrow.

'Other things seem to have got in the way.'

'Samoa tends to be like that. Vould you be so kind, my friend, as to pass me that shirt?'

A purple shirt, shot through with silver, hangs on another bush. Guy steps across, picks up the shirt, hands it to Wolfgang. My head is pounding. The heat. The bloody birds screaming. Mosquitoes biting.

'I'm still inclined to give the land to Mr Bismarck,' falters Guy. 'We may not feel very warmly towards the gentleman in question but Bertie's last verbal wishes, even if contrary to his written testament, must be paramount, I think?'

Wolfgang nods thoughtfully.

Oh for heaven's sake – time for me to speak out!

'Guy, he's got no right to it,' I say. 'We should put the land on the market, convert it into cash – and if you're really and truly bent on an act of charity, why kowtow to someone so crotchety, why not give the money to a local school or orphanage instead of handing it over to an ugly bully?'

Wolfgang, having tugged the purple shirt over his torso and straightened his ponytail, looks my way.

'Bertie Blandvood did not believe Stevenson Bismarck to be an ugly bully, my dear lady. She believed he vas good and loving.'

I slap at a mosquito haplessly.

'She – he – Bertie – had quite likely lost all touch with reality, Mr Wanderer. How bound are we to obey the wishes of someone perhaps no longer fully competent to make decisions?'

The bright little eyes of the lawyer now look at me in a newly pointed way.

'Missy Bertie vas not insane,' he says slowly.

'Oh, I wasn't quite meaning – '

'Nobody upon their deathbed vas ever more sane than Bertram Blandvood of Paradise in Heaven.'

Guy looks nowhere awkwardly.

'I hope,' he says, 'to look at the land again today, as we arranged, and make up my mind after talking some more with Mr Bismarck.'

I slap another mosquito.

I can't bear the thought of trailing out again to that dreadful spot.

'Guysie,' I say, 'perhaps I won't go after all – I think it might be best for me not to go but to stay.'

He looks at me a bit blankly.

'Well, darling – ' he says, 'if you're not keen – '

'It'll be so horribly hot and glaring out there and you don't really need me, do you sweetheart?' I go on, aware that my voice has veered close to whining. 'I'll just go back to the hotel and spend the day by the pool with the odd gin and tonic.'

'Of course, darling – ' he starts to say.

Wolfgang, however, sees things quite another way.

'Pru, you must come!' he almost barks. 'Guy is the heir but you are Guy's right arm – this I know, from vatching the two of you – you are half your husband's heart, half his soul – and the land, this land of vich ve are speaking – this land has a heart, too – this land has a soul, too.'

'A heart is an organ for pumping blood, Mr Wanderer,' I snap. 'Land is dirt and rock – mostly rock, in the case of Paradise in Heaven.'

'Would it be too tiresome for you, Pwu?' says Guy, levelling his eyes on mine somewhat longingly.

The poor old boy.

'Sweetheart, of course I'll come if it means so much to you.'

'Always trumps, darling.'

I now feel guilt. A quick stab. Tui.

'Thanks, sweetheart.'

'Vell, now ve go there and have our talk vith Stevenson and see vhether or not any new feelings emerge, or old feelings shape up more coherently, or just to pay honour to Bertie's memory. Paradise in Heaven may not look much chop to you, Pru, but that little spot made Bertie so happy. She loved it deeply. I remember the first time I met our dear Bertie,' – he waves us in a dishevelled yet gallant sort of way towards a tumbledown car shed – 'and how she was thin and bewildered and single, vearing men's clothes, looking hot and itchy in a vite linen suit, and had come to me to handle the papervork for buying Paradise in Heaven.'

'A white linen suit would look a little more fitting than that ghastly outfit in the photo on his grave,' I say. 'And as soon as he stepped off the plane someone should have binned every bit of henna in Samoa.'

'She came by sea, not by air, my dear Pru,' says Wolfgang.

The car inside the shed is a battered old Volkswagen. I, having short legs, find myself squeezed into the back.

Wolfgang, grating gears, begins driving.

Coconut palms, banana trees, breadfruit trees. Shanties, shops. Women dawdling. Kids playing. Kids throwing stones at dogs. Pigs. Poultry. Nothing has become less a dive and more a lovely haven since our first day.

Nor, it turns out, has Paradise in Heaven.

The savannah grass is still spiky. The waves still slap listlessly onto black lava lumps. The thatched roof over the wooden deck still looks like a broken umbrella. Stevenson stalks towards us, scowling.

'Paradise in Heaven is not your land!' he says by way of welcome. 'This land is for me, for me and memory.'

Wolfgang spills out something in Samoan. I watch silently.

'We're here,' says Guy, 'to learn your point of view, Mr Bismarck.'

Stevenson keeps scowling. A dirty little dog, backed onto its haunches, begins snarling. Wolfgang keeps spilling out more words in Samoan. The sound of the language seems sometimes like water. Water flowing. Wolfgang does seem to have the gift of the gab. Stevenson, while listening intently, is fingering those sickening machete scars on his neck. He seems to be softening. After a bit he glances almost gently at Guy. We find ourselves being welcomed into the fale, though that means nothing more than climbing a few steps onto the wooden deck. Woven mats on the deck have been swept. Bedding has been rolled up neatly. No chairs. No tables. Nothing but a few wooden boxes and an old steamer trunk. Bertie must have lived very plainly.

Mosquitoes find my arms and legs.

I start slapping.

'That's me!' I hear Guy say suddenly.

He's looking at a glazed and framed photo of a boy. The photo – only a snap really but wreathed with flowers – has been hung from a post. Yes, the boy in the photo is my poor sweetheart when he was about ten years old. A worried boy. The snap looks like it was taken on the driveway at Whitepark.

Stevenson looks narrowly at Guy.

Wolfgang gargles Samoan words. Stevenson gargles back, and goes on gargling. After quite some time, he stops.

'Missy Bertie alvays insisted that fresh garlands be hung around this photograph,' says Wolfgang. 'Stevenson has kept it garlanded accordingly.'

'I – I really – ' says Guy.

'Missy Bertie,' goes on Wolfgang, 'told our friend that the photograph shows the one person she loved in her family.'

Stevenson looks at Guy.

'So you that little boy?' he says.

'Yes,' says Guy. 'I'm that little boy.'

Stevenson astonishes all three of us by stepping straight across to my poor darling and giving him a big smacking kiss. A kiss on the mouth! Guy, blushing, looks away. He steps back. Stevenson, stepping further forward, lifts an oily brown hand and caresses my poor old boy's cheek tenderly.

'Come!' he cries. 'Come, I show you everything!'

Wolfgang is grinning.

Guy, guided by a strong grip on his elbow, gets steered off the deck. Stevenson starts yammering about the land, the sea, the fishing. I make a move to trail along, sticky and sweaty and decidedly de trop.

Stevenson glares at me sternly.

'You! It's hot for you. Stay in the fale. Sit on a mat!'

I bridle a bit, not knowing whether to try giving him some sort of comeuppance. Actually, though, who wants to follow the men out into the heat? I'll stay in the shade, thank you. So I do. I sit on a mat. I set down my handbag. I close my eyes. I try not to mind the mosquitoes. I listen to the sounds of the land. Swishing. Buzzing. Humming. Now and then a few words spoken by the men are blown in by a breeze from the bay. I'm nodding off. Nodding off while keeping one eye cocked for spiders, which may well be poisonous, and also fat furry centipedes which I know are certainly poisonous.

I jolt awake when I hear footsteps.

Stevenson has leapt onto the deck of the fale. Guy comes clambering up alongside. Stevenson wraps a sinewy arm around my poor boy's shoulder, squeezes him hard and begins whispering.

'I don't like that your wife. Cold lady. Very cold lady.'

The cheek of the bloody man. I'm not cold anyway. I'm sopping with bloody sweat in the bloody heat!

'At least,' I say, sitting up very straight, 'have the good grace not to slander me when I'm within earshot.'

Guy smiles awkwardly.

Stevenson, ignoring my protest, once more squeezes Guy.

'I want to warm you. You throw her away and be my little wife, me and you together in Paradise in Heaven.'

Guy looks so shocked and scared it's clear that he'd be quite keen to jump up, run away and very likely not stop running. I almost burst out laughing. I bite my lower lip instead, pretty sure laughter won't be what he wants to hear from me right now.

'You're very kind, Stevenson,' he says, meticulously picking his words. 'However, you need to know that my marriage is happy and also that I'm a father.'

Stevenson looks at him lovingly.

'I am a father too,' he says. 'Seven children in three villages.'

Guy looks at me wildly.

'Yes, but – but – ,' he stammers. 'No, no, I'm not that way.'

Stevenson pats Guy.

'You think, think a lot. I waiting for you. I am a very good husband for you.'

Wolfgang, who seems to have been keeping himself busy by walking in the village, comes back chatting with some urchins. I wonder whether among those urchins is the one who landed the stone on my forehead during on our first day. I don't seem to care, really. I close my eyes. I hear the bass and baritone of the men while they keep on speaking. I hear the treble chattering of the urchins. I open my eyes.

I see the weatherbeaten plank with its weary red words.

Paradise in Heaven.

Wolfgang after a while leads us back to his old bomb and drives us away. Guy holds my hand. We've settled nothing about the land. Shacks and chooks go by. Wolfgang begins humming. I know the tune. It's that old peace song from the eighties, *Neunundneunzig Luftballons*. Guy begins humming too. Stones are kicked up by our wheels. We get to the main road. Our little motor is whining.

I close my eyes, start snoozing.

Flowers opening soft scarlet sticky love yellow love brown boy glossy limbs dark eyes kiss lick love lonely –

'Pwu,' murmurs Guy.

'Mmmm?'

We're back at Queen Lupe's, getting our keys from the front desk. A letter is waiting. A letter on good paper stamped with the red and blue and gold of the national coat of arms headed with the address of our High Commission. Opening it, we find an invitation for dinner the evening after tomorrow.

'Well, that's thoughtful,' says Guy.

'Do we need to go, though, sweetheart?'

'I think I'd rather not bother, if you don't mind darling?'

'I quite categorically would rather not bother. I wonder why not?'

We gaze at each other and seem not to see anything like an answer in each other's eyes. I'm aware that neither of us has said anything yet about getting a new phone. I did think this morning that it might make sense to get one of our old phones sent over here from home by courier. You know, to save us the bother of going the round of shops here trying to find a decent model and the further bother of tracking down our numbers. Now, though – well –

'Are we going troppo, do you think?' tries Guy. 'Going off the deep end, like Bertie?'

'Sweetheart, you'd look lovely in a beehive hairdo and cerise lipstick.'

The way he seems to blanch, then look away, is not so surprising. The dear old thing never has been wholly at home with even the littlest bit of teasing. I suppose, too, that having a transvestite uncle can hardly be the easiest thing to swallow even for someone who on the whole won't allow himself to be cowed by what the world might say or think about his family.

He writes a polite note turning down the dinner invitation, after which we settle by the pool with drinks.

A white wine for Guy. A gin and tonic for me. The water in the pool slaps idly. Dead beetles float on top. We talk about what to do next. Wolfgang has suggested we go away for another beach stay. I'm not sure, frankly. I want to get shot of Samoa. At the same time, I did love the lagoon at Teuila Villas. And we're here. And my poor boy wants a few more days or a week or two to keep thinking about what to do with Paradise in Heaven. Hock in his hand, he says again that the best thing might be just to give it to Stevenson. Oily gin in my hand, I say that it's the principle of the thing.

'A right to land ownership is a right to land ownership. You should know that. After all, you're the one who was in the law.'

'Right. A tricky word. Often a synonym for wrong.'

'Right is right and left is left and wrong is wrong, isn't it?'

'Hmm, well back to the question at hand, apparently there are some pleasant beach resorts on the south coast of Upolu. I was wondering whether this time we might try somewhere still simpler than Teuila Villas.'

'I don't mind. Shall we go to the tourist office for advice?'

'Or we could have a thorough talk about it with Wolfgang. He knows the lie of the land.'

'Sweetheart, he's such an old – *hippy*! Won't he want us to go somewhere ghastly? You know, composting lavs, the whiff of cannabis and lots of people from the wrong suburbs of Christchurch and Auckland.'

Guy laughs.

'Wolfgang seems to me a pretty shrewd judge of character. He'll know what we're needing.'

We eat a light lunch by the pool. Afterwards, my poor old boy sets off for a long walk while I snuggle down in my suite for more snoozing. After quite a while I wake up, freshen myself and walk out through the steamy heat of late afternoon to a little park where groups of people are seated looking at other groups of people. Looking stolidly, and mostly silently. Samoans seem to do a lot of sitting and staring. I gaze from side to side, wondering whether to keep walking or give up because of the heat, when I see two white women sloping along.

The women are about my age. One is stout and square, her red hair shaved back to a sort of bristly skullcap. A pink lavalava flaps around her blotchy ankles. The other is thin and bony, her hair azure blue and fluffy. Short green shorts flap around her blotchy thighs. The two women are looking everywhere alertly.

Should I turn away, making out I haven't seen?

'Girls!' I call out. 'Lynne! Sandy!'

The sisters, stopping in their tracks, their coarse honest faces creasing with friendliness, come scooting across. I wonder why I'm so keen to see the twosome again as they grab me heartily and smack smooches on my cheeks.

'Gidday Pru,' says Lynne.

'How ya going?' adds Sandy.

'Oh, you know – enjoying this sea breeze, girls. Did you scatter the ashes successfully?'

'Act of filial piety ticked off list!' says Lynne. 'Mum's ashes flung over hallowed ground as per plan! Right now we're bloody hungry. Our hotel dining room's no good. So we were just wondering where to eat when who should flag us down but our buddy from the cold old South Island. What's the kai like at your pub, Pru?'

'So-so,' I say, then stop to think. 'And – well – '

A bit pricey, I was going to say. The sisters no doubt need to count pretty much every penny. I think better of saying so. I have a brainwave. They're looking for food. I'm a bit – lost?

I'll give the two of them a treat!

'Why not come and be my guests? We can get ourselves settled with a drink and order room service and take things easy.'

'Well that's bloody nice of you, Pru,' says Lynne. 'I'm in!'

'Same,' says Sandy.

The three of us are soon sunk inside the cane steamer chairs on my private terrace and the sisters are poking around in their handbags for their reading glasses so they can swot up the menu for room service.

'Go to town, girls,' I say. 'It's on me.'

At first they jib because of the prices, saying they don't want to sponge, but if there's one thing I've been trained to do well it's courteously forcing guests to accept lavish hospitality. Next comes a lot of excited whooping over the menu and the drinks list. Afterwards, having phoned through our orders, I open a bottle of chardonnay. The sisters ask whether I've been enjoying my holiday. I look out at waving coconut palms while doing my best to gather my wits. The temptation is to answer with a few white lies, which is what I'd do if I were asked the question by the vicar or my mother or Buffy. Yet, for some reason – some reason a bit beyond me – I feel I owe these two the truth.

'I've done something a little out of character,' I say quietly.

The girls look at me keenly.

I can't quite go on.

'Yeah?' prompts Lynne.

'Out of character, for me, I mean,' I say a little less quietly, a little more firmly. 'I had a – well – a bit of a fling.'

I wait to see how the girls take this. They take it well. No shock, no ogling, no leering.

'You don't have to talk about it if you don't want,' says Lynne.

'Though better out than in, to my mind,' prompts Sandy.

'Oh, it's all been pretty disastrous, girls. And between us three, a fling with a young man.'

'Shit!' laughs Lynne. 'And what's so disastrous about that?'

'I'm not sure,' I say with a sudden need to cry, which I fight back. 'I've been taken for a fool. He was just after money. And it's made me feel – I feel as though – I feel as though I'm suddenly without bearings, as though the earth beneath my feet has shifted. I feel as though here is there, and there is here, and – and it frightens me. I don't know what to do. I wonder whether the best thing would be to go away from here – go away from here and get myself back home to Canterbury.'

'Nah,' says Sandy. 'I reckon it is what it is.'

'Don't overthink it,' says Lynne.

I feel a bit better, somehow, for having spoken out. The three of us sit silent for a tick or two. We look towards the setting sun. Next thing the sisters start talking about the sights, and about snorkelling, and then about the taste and texture of taro leaf cooked in coconut milk. I'm chiming in by now. We talk about tapa. We talk about pigs. We talk about dogs. We talk about sheet lightning seen offshore last night.

'Where's your hubby got himself to – having a few at the bar, is he?' asks Lynne. 'Men, eh!'

'Oh, possibly,' I say.

'Doesn't leave much of a mark, does he? Not like most blokes. Underpants everywhere. You'd hardly know anyone, let alone a man, was bunked up in here with you.'

I feel a bit awkward. On the other hand, why should I bother feeling awkward? Who, after all, are Lynne and Sandy? A brace of nice but brassy office workers from Auckland! A couple of workaday women who know nobody I know – who never will know anybody I know. I take the plunge and speak openly.

'He's got his own rooms. We don't like sharing a bed.'

The sisters glance at each other before I get a grin from Lynne.

'Nice work if you can get it! Quick visits for tomfoolery every night or so and then the luxury of the whole bed to yourself!'

'Actually, the two of us,' I start slowly, not sure whether to keep going. 'You know, Guy and I – '

The sisters go quiet.

'I mean to say, Guy and I – '

Oh dear.

'Yeah?' says Lynne.

'You and Guy?' says Sandy.

Well, how can it hurt to talk? How can it be anything but helpful to open my heart – to talk about it to two women who're nobodies and know nobody?

'Guy and I,' I say, my words coming out in what sounds surprisingly like a croak. 'We've – well, we've not had sex for a very long time.'

'Aw, okay,' says Lynne, looking at me more soberly.

'I know it's normal enough, of course,' I soldier on. 'You know, when you clock up a few years of wedlock.'

I seem, now, to see all those years of wedlock in a dull orderly dutiful row.

Lynne looks at me still more soberly.

'We're probably just a crowd of sex maniacs in our family,' she says, picking her words, 'but even when my Arnold was half in his grave I was still at him for a root.'

Sandy ducks her azure head.

'Sex maniacs is right,' she says. 'Cause even though I divorced my Gavin – cause we didn't get on too good – I've really missed getting my leg over.'

'How long have you and Guy been married, Pru?' chips in Lynne.

I tell them how long.

'Aw, mmm,' says Sandy.

'How long did you stay with Gavin then, Sandy?'

'Thirty years before I cleared away that wasted space, Pru.'

'I see.'

A waiter knocks. A trolley laden with dishes – and deliverance – gets rolled through the suite and out onto the terrace. The sisters tuck in with gusto. We talk about our youngsters. Sandy has sons and a daughter in Auckland and Queensland. Lynne has daughters and a son in Queensland and Auckland. They both look a bit stumped by my sketch of Charley in London and Tim in Hong Kong. We talk about youngsters as a whole. We talk about youngsters in Samoa. We talk about women in

Samoa. We talk about women as a whole. We swing onto politics before grasping – swiftly! – that we'd better steer away.

I think this may well be the first time in my life I've broken bread with anybody who votes for the Labour Party.

The sisters, after tucking away a last wine or two, lunge at me with hugs. I don't want them to go. Somehow it's as though the three of us have gone somewhere together, somewhere new to me yet not new to them, clearly.

They do go, though.

'You look after yourself, Pru,' says Lynne, giving me one more hearty hug.

'I've loved meeting you both,' I say, oddly. 'You're two out of the box.'

'Well that makes three of us then!' booms Sandy. 'We most likely are sex maniacs, so don't – you know, worry.'

They trot away.

Dropping myself back onto one of the steamer chairs and looking out at the deepening night, I mull for a bit about the two. Office workers from Auckland! And then I mull about myself. Why have I never talked about sex with anybody? I've joked about it, of course – quick remarks, ostensibly witty, tossed back and forth over dinner tables – chance observations at country fetes, gymkhanas – but never – never exposing myself, never speaking the truth about what's happened – or not happened – with me, with Guy. I don't suppose what the two sisters got up to with their husbands was so very out of the ordinary.

Guy and I – are we the ones who're out of the ordinary?

Are most married couples at it hammer and tongs?

Perhaps it's my fault for being too – passive? Perhaps I should have been seducing him with naughty knickers? Only he'd still – well, he'd still be Guy, I mean, not exactly a brooding hero. Perhaps I should have – given up? You know, left him!

Oh how silly.

Mount Silisili.

I'm utterly at sixes and sevens. Can't seem to think straight in this horrible heat – this sticky sweaty smelly little city – this rotten little country. I'd give anything for a nice crisp Canterbury frost!

CHAPTER TWELVE

The two of us flinch a bit upon first sighting the fales at Sina ma le Tuna Resort. Wooden posts have been driven into the sand. Decks of roughly dressed planks sit on top. Other wooden posts hold up roofs of palm thatch and corrugated iron. Planks, nailed onto the roof posts, climb to my neck height to make a sort of fence around each deck. One can make the back private by lowering a few rickety blinds. The blinds, like so many other things on these islands, have been made from palm fronds. The front half of each deck is a veranda with a wooden balustrade and two rough wooden chairs, nearly as rickety as the blinds.

'If not for the white and yellow paint that's been splashed about,' I say to Guy, 'it'd be hard to tell them apart from that shanty of Bertie's.'

'A pretty spot, though, darling,' he says in reply.

We're standing on gleaming sand, a dazzling strand. Waves clap. Palms sway. We can see a little island, deep green and jungled, hovering above the lagoon. I screw up my eyes behind my pointlessly fashionable sunglasses.

'I suppose so,' I confess reluctantly. 'It's rather – well, really it's rather lovely.'

'I think it's even lovelier than Teuila Villas.'

'Mm?'

The inside of my fale is like the inside of a wicker picnic basket. Blinds and thatch creak and rattle in a warm breeze off the lagoon. Quickly unpacking my bag, I hum a song while hanging things on nails. The nails are rusty and someone not too skilled has hammered them into the wall posts. My housekeeping seen to, I step back out onto my veranda and look down towards the lagoon. Guy has begun wandering along the sand. He looks lonely. A group of young brown men are raking the sand. A group of old white people are starting to go red from sunning themselves on brilliantly hued beach towels. A family has begun playing beach cricket, a towheaded white family whose accent tells me they come from Southland.

I sit on my veranda, in bare feet and cotton shorts, watching.

The young men raking the sand are slim, sleek, glistening with sweat. One looks like an elf, his black hair curly.

Guy, wandering back, gives me a wave and not long afterwards climbs up my steps.

'*Very* nice spot, this, don't you think Pru?'

'It does seem to have a good – what's the word? Mood? A good mood.'

The towheaded family on the sand dashes laughingly into the lagoon and starts splashing.

'Pru, why did we never play beach cricket on a tropical island with Tim and Charley?'

'Well – '

I think about the days we spent with the offs on the beaches of Banks Peninsula and Provence and the Algarve and Abel Tasman National Park. Charley never seemed to enjoy herself on sand. She complained it made everything gritty. Tim complained too. Beaches, he said, were boring.

'Why did we never play anything at all with Tim and Charley?'

'We *did*, Guy! We took them to pony club. We took them skiing. We worked damned hard to do our best by them.'

'Did we?'

A soft dinning echoes up and down the sand. The lunch gong. We soon find ourselves seated on a big wooden deck next to the family from Southland. A pleasant family. The mother and father are about forty and in the law, practising in Invercargill. They talk shop with Guy. Food and drinks are served by smiling young men who pad backwards and forwards with strong springy strides. On their hips hang the green and turquoise lavalava worn by staff at Sina ma le Tuna. The young man handing food to our table is the one who looks like an elf.

'Thank you,' I say. 'And what's your name?'

'Karl,' says the boy.

'I'm Pru, and this is my husband, Guy.'

'So please to meet you. You from Niu Sila?'

'Yes, New Zealand,' I say. 'Are you from this village?'

'Nex village. I'm love Niu Sila. It's mus be the rich peoples they live there.'

Chat, more chat, till by the end of the meal I've swapped affable words with three others of the staff while also getting along comfortably with the Southlanders. The food is agreeable, too. A lot of fresh fish caught by the men from the village, together with fruit and a tasty dish made from coconut milk and taro shoots. Guy and I each drink a glass of the light local lager. Afterwards we sit on the beach looking out at the breakers on the reef.

'I have nightmares about the breakers on the reefs here in Samoa,' I tell Guy.

'Do you, darling? What sort of nightmares are they?'

'Hard to say. A sort of feeling that the reefs are supposed to keep me safe, but then suddenly one huge breaker goes right over the top. Goes right over the top and – and comes for me!'

'You feel frightened?'

'Very. Helpless.'

'Does the wave get you?'

'Not quite – not yet! I wake up.'

'I think I read somewhere that dreaming about waves has nothing to do with one's emotions and only mirrors alterations in one's body temperature while one's sleeping.'

'Well, that's reassuring. Apropos of sleeping, snooze time for me now.'

'Sweet dreams, darling. I'll go for a walk.'

The dreams aren't sweet. I toss and turn for an hour or so. And snort and snore, I dare say. I wake up. I yawn, stand, stretch, rinse my mouth with water and a dash of eau de cologne and wrap myself in my lavalava. You know, the lavalava I bought on our first day in Apia. The violet lavalava with flowers in lime green, crude but pretty. The lavalava that shamed me by falling to the concrete floor at the ferry terminal. I open my flimsy front door and step out onto my little veranda. A kingfisher sits among the glossy leaves of a nearby tree. I look at the glassy waters of the lagoon.

'Please love me, somebody,' I hear myself whispering.

I go for a bit of a walk.

A walk towards the end of the beach, which is no great distance, a kilometre or so. The plinking sound of a guitar draws my gaze towards a fale whose blinds have not been lowered and inside which I see a tangle of resting boys. Karl, the young man with the curls who served us our lunch, sits crosslegged wearing nothing but a lavalava. He's the one playing the guitar. Another young man has twined an arm around his shoulder and hums gently. Two other boys, locked in an embrace on top of a pink mattress, are sleeping. A last boy sits on the steps.

'Talofa,' I say.

'Where are you going?' comes the reply.

I know, now, that this question is not really a question but a greeting.

The way the boys have draped themselves over one another is charming. Charming and of course arousing. I mustn't allow myself to feel aroused, however, mustn't allow erotic visions involving any of these innocent lads to twist themselves into my ageing, older, over-the-hill skull.

Tui.

I go to the end of the beach, look at waves breaking white on the reef, then walk back to Sina ma le Tuna. I step on to my veranda. I open my flimsy front door. I drop myself back on my bed. I close my eyes. I close my mind.

I sleep.

'Nice nap, Pwu?' asks Guy upon my second awakening.

He's seated on the matting next to my bed. I note, once more, that his mood seems less than buoyant.

'Dead to the world, Guysie.'

We make a few remarks about the stillness, the heat. I get up, take another swig of water.

'I wonder, am I really like Bertie?' says Guy. 'Stevenson said so.'

'Does it matter, darling?'

'I suppose not. Swim now, sweetheart?'

'Gin now, sweetheart.'

Drink proves to be my downfall that evening. After dinner, and a coffee with the couple from Southland, the hours begin to hang somewhat heavy. Guy takes himself and a book off to bed by nine and I find myself dawdling up and down the beach. I go, at last, to a rocky point where a sort of ledge looks out over the silken dark waters of the lagoon. On getting to the ledge, I find five of the boys from the resort seated crosslegged and taking sips from a bottle of vodka. The bottle, grasped by each hand in turn, winks in the moonlight. One of the boys is Karl.

'Where are you going?' he says.

'To join your party,' I say.

'Awesome!'

Amazed at my boldness, I seat myself alongside them on the ledge. Karl's knee jostles me in a friendly way. He passes me the vodka. I take a swig. I pass on the vodka. The boys begin singing.

I don't know the song.

The boys are pretty drunk by the time several songs have been sung. I note two empty vodka bottles stowed under a rock. Karl turns to me, leans forward, smiling. His brown chest is thin yet sinewy.

'You are the so beauty one,' he says. 'All the boys are looking for your arse.'

What? Clearly he's having me on – *my* podgy arse, I ask you!

'You're so handsome,' I say. 'I love your curls.'

He looks at me, puzzled. I think it's not a word he knows. Curls.

'Let's sex,' he says.

Golly – that was quick!

He stands, like a young prince, and touches one of my haggard cheeks. His fingertips trace little arabesques. I feel myself melting. I jump up. I snatch at his hand. A strong, strong hand. Oh goodness me, what a – what an overwhelming muddle of feelings. The other boys are looking away tactfully. I wonder whether every young man on these islands is trying to get into bed with – well, into the purse of – every old white woman? Quite clearly whatever's happening is pretty much par for the course with resort boys.

I tug at Karl.

'Come on,' I say. 'Come with me.'

I keep tugging his hand, more or less dragging him across the rocks and around a bit of a spur where I soon spy out a spot in darkness. I scuttle to the spot. Karl follows. I stop. He stops. I touch his chest. I breathe his smell. I bend my head back. He kisses me. I slip my tongue between his lips. So wonderful to feel that I can let myself go. Wonderful to know that he's only some libidinous boy looking for fun, no more and no less. Wonderful to know that he's not serious, not a man, not someone I need to flatter or impress or manage or – I can just be myself, I can seek whatever I want – and I can get it!

I unbutton my blouse, unhook my bra, push his head down to my breasts.

He suckles greedily.

Blissful, blissful. I make sure he's there for a while before letting him slide me down onto a flat rock – well, flattish – and lower himself on top. I push his head down between my legs. I wrap my legs around his neck – also something I've never done before – blissful – blissful!

'Now I want you to fuck me,' I say.

I've never told any man I wanted him to fuck me – not so bluntly. I feel powerful. He's keen to obey, throwing aside his lavalava, sliding inside me, slowly starting to rock in and out. I understand, suddenly, that's not what I want. I push him back off me. He looks shocked.

'Lie down on your back,' I say.

He smiles, and does so.

I sit astride him – which is also something I've never done before – lower myself down on him – oh my god, who is this confident woman? Who's this – this slut? A slut whose bottom is white and flabby. A quick wave of shame – thinking about that whiteness, that flabbiness – before more bliss. Bliss at feeling the forceful grip of his brown stubby fingers. Bliss at being a woman riding a young man. What would they say at the vestry? Jim of course would make allusions to horses mating. Buffy, I imagine, would look prunelike but secretly be envious. Also, of course, there's Mummy. Perhaps terriers have more fun than greyhounds?

My mind flips back to Karl, whose face is contorting and whose grip is tightening. God, he's going to climax – he *is* climaxing.

Oh no, far too soon!

Whilst feeling very powerful for having brought him off so quickly, I'm also vexed. I need more. Lifting myself up, rolling off him, I lie on my back.

'Now make me climax,' I say, once more pushing down his head.

He complies.

Bliss, bliss – bliss!

Fuck, fuck, fuck, fuck, fuck!

Afterwards, he asks about tomorrow night. I tell him I'll see how I'm feeling and then send him packing. I'm proud of myself for being so cool. I sit on the flat rock for a bit longer, listening to the soft sounds of the night. The heave of the lagoon. The breeze in the palms.

A twinge of two of awkward feelings get in my way for a short while when I go back to my fale, lower the flimsy blinds – they drop with a rustling rattle – and climb into bed. Yet suddenly any awkwardness is forgotten and I'm fast asleep and I'm dreaming happy dreams about handsome brown boys, and flabby white bottoms, and bliss. Bliss, boys – boys, bliss.

Curiously enough, I awaken next morning at break of day. Guy finds me swimming when he comes out of his own fale after he, as usual, also gets up early. The water in the lagoon is a beautiful cyan blue. He runs towards me across the sand. He dives under the wavelets. We tease and laugh and splash each other and carry on like a couple of kids.

'Nice to see you enjoying yourself, Pwu,' he says as we towel ourselves off on the sand.

'It's a *lovely* spot,' I say a bit sheepishly.

'It is,' he says.

I turn sideways, take a look at him, and see he's smiling – smiling widely.

'You're perking up, Guysie. I was worrying about you a bit. You were looking a bit – well, low.'

He stops smiling and looks out to sea.

'Samoa grows on me, or so I find,' he says.

'Well to be perfectly honest, darling, it grows on me too.'

A group of brown young men come sauntering across the sand. Karl, one of the group, catches my eye. He winks. I wince. The wince and wink aren't obvious, however, because the other boys are smiling and waving at us too. The tallest among the group is carrying two rugby balls, one of which he suddenly lobs – after stopping in his tracks, lifting a right arm, a very muscled right arm – lobbing it towards Guy. My poor darling catches it with two hands and lobs it back to the tall boy.

'Man, les go!' yells one of the other boys.

'Where are you going?' I call out.

'We're go for the walk,' the tall boy calls back. 'Walking walking.'

Off they go, lavalavas loosening and tightening across their thick thighs, their breathtaking buttocks.

'Laauli, that's his name, isn't it – the boy with the balls?' I ask Guy.

'I think so,' he answers, ducking his head.

'Such nice boys, aren't they?' I feel game enough to say.

'Very nice boys,' agrees Guy.

He's smiling again – smiling widely again – which causes my guilt to kick in and make me fidgety. Afterwards, having walked back to my fale, I lie wondering under the mosquito net. Breakfast follows. The low morning light, striking the surface of the lagoon, shoots glittering shafts into our eyes. Mosquitoes get busy. Guy talks to the lawyers from Southland about the trees and shrubs of Samoa.

'Interesting,' says the lawyer wife, 'how so many native species of woody flowering plant here look to be quite closely related to our own native species of woody flowering plant.'

'Interesting indeed,' says Guy. 'I've noted the relationship myself on my walks.'

'I wonder whether it's a consequence of seaborne or airborne seeding,' says the lawyer husband. 'Or whether it goes back to Gondwanaland.'

'I imagine more the former than the latter,' says my poor old wordy sweetheart. 'Given that Samoa has come up above the water thanks to volcanic activity, while orogeny is the key factor in New Zealand.'

'The two closely linked, of course,' adds the wife.

'Of course,' agrees Guy.

I keep quiet, mostly.

After a last coffee we wander back to our fales, potter about for a bit, go swimming, sun ourselves, go swimming again. Guy and I sit together on my veranda drinking tea while reading – or rather, Guy reads while I feign reading. Karl, at one point, pads past with a carton for the kitchen and gives me another wink. Guy, luckily, has his nose in his book.

'Fiafia this evening, evidently,' I say. 'It'll be a bit of fun, one hopes.'

'Not a *bit* of fun,' says Guy. 'A *lot* of fun, I'm sure, darling.'

'You're so cheery today, sweetheart.'

'Sorry.'

'No, no – it's lovely.'

A fiafia is a sort of evening concert to be put on by the young men and women of the hotel staff. Awareness of the upcoming festivity seems to make the day go languorously. I don't anticipate much from the fiafia, mind you. A bit of singing. A bit of dancing. I'm dreaming of getting off alone once more with Karl. Dinner comes. Dinner goes. After dinner, we all gather on the social deck. A few men begin to play drums and guitars. Young women, wreathed with greenery, start twisting their feet and twining their arms in a graceful sort of way. Young men, also wreathed with greenery, move strenuously. Sweat springs up. All the young people are smiling. All the guests are smiling and clapping.

Guy and I have seated ourselves once more with the lawyers, who no longer canvass the native trees and shrubs of Samoa but instead the native trees and shrubs of Southland and Canterbury.

'I think the Southland lax leaf is the most marvellous variant of cordyline australis,' says Guy.

I'm drinking a nice enough white wine, a pinot gris.

'No no,' says the lawyer wife. 'Your wharanui variant in Canterbury is so elegant!'

I'm drinking a tad too much, really.

'It's elegant, I agree,' drones on my old boy. 'The lavish branching of your lax leaf, though – well it's simply extraordinary.'

The lawyer couple beam at Guy.

Guy beams back.

'The waiters are a bit lazy this evening, aren't they?' I say. 'I've been trying to catch the eye of one so I can get another drink.'

'Let me go up to the bar, darling,' says Guy, bending towards me gallantly.

'Don't worry, I'll go,' I reply, patting his hand – secretly keen as mustard to get up, get away.

Leaping to my feet, flashing what I hope looks like a friendly smile at everyone, I weave barwards, perhaps a trifle boozily. I skirt the bar, however, and head instead towards a big breadfruit out the back. I know, from having already made a sly reconnaissance, that somewhere behind the breadfruit I'll find Karl.

CHAPTER THIRTEEN

Karl crouches over a drum whose skin he's busy stretching. A crude yellow light, cast by a naked bulb, makes his forehead look oily, too massive, while his eyes look black, lost. He looks up. The eyes become doe eyes.

'Tonight we can sex in the fale,' he whispers. 'Lotsa sex in the fale.'

My heart starts beating quickly.

'I'm not sure,' I whisper back. 'I don't know – my husband, Guy – '

He grins – or is it a smirk?

'I know you love me,' he says.

'Yes!' I blurt out, just to keep in my hand, given that this is most likely some sort of game.

He looks into my eyes.

'I see you at your fale in five minutes.'

He strides off, leaving behind the drum. I stand under the breadfruit. What on earth – ? How *did* all this start happening? Swivelling on the spot, looking beyond the shining oiled pillars of the social deck, I watch the luscious lad loping across the sand.

What shall I do?

Of course I'm not going to have some sort of tryst with him inside my fale. It'd be worse than foolish to do something so openly. I mean to say – well, while very likely none of the other guests would see anything, or pay any heed if they did see anything, what about Guy? And the staff? I'm pretty sure that the staff see everything, understand everything. Close observation of everything and everybody must be a key skill for anybody trying to navigate their way through village life here in Samoa.

Not so very unlike life in country townships back home, really.

I look across at Guy.

The poor boy is still earnestly droning. I imagine he may well have begun spelling out, now, why he's never been convinced by the classification of cordyline australis. Or something along those lines. Guy, when he's got himself firmly saddled on top of one of his hobby horses, will happily go on for an hour or even more. And the couple from Southland seem quite as happy to keep it up.

Karl's grin – a smile, or a smirk?

Perhaps I should?

No, I can't, it's too risky! Yet my sozzled noggin seems to be screening a private show behind my eyes, a show featuring a sinewy brown chest, a taut brown abdomen, bulging brown calves –

So perhaps – ?

I go to the bar, buy a neat whisky, knock it back in one go.

Drifting towards the steps, dawdling down the steps, straying as though aimlessly across the sand, I'm soon outside my fale. He's waiting. Karl. He's seated in a chair on my veranda. A bright little light in each of his eyes. Oh dear, I'm still not entirely clear what I'm going to do. Karl stands. He opens the fale door – which I've left unlocked. He steps inside straightaway – steps purposefully, before I have a chance to take one step forward or back. I follow. The inside of the fale is dark. I make up my mind to keep it dark. He's stripping off his shirt, showing me in the looming gloom that, yes, the brown chest is still thin but sinewy and, yes, the brown abdomen has stayed taut.

He drops onto my bed, unfolding his long body.

I drop onto the bed, too.

'At home I have my two sisters and my two brothers and my nephews and my nieces,' he says afterwards when we're lying side by side under the mosquito net. 'My mum pass away.'

'Do you stay with your dad?'

I've learned during the last few weeks that Samoans when speaking English don't use the verb live but instead the verb stay.

'He stay with the other part of my family. He's not drinking. He's not smoking. He keep on sending money. Not handsome! He's a Samoa but he looks like a Tonga. He's going to work for the banana.'

I think he means his father works on a banana plantation.

'Are you a happy family?'

'Happy. All happy. I stay with my aunty. Aunty call us shit and pig and chase us with the broom and hit us hardhard. One of my brother he working in Niu Sila. And one of my brother he staying at Apia. He's my best brother. He give me good advices. He don't punch me, even though he get angry sometimes. Most of the families, they do that.'

'Punch each other?'

'Yeah. One of my sister has black marks. She get the marks because she fight with one of my neighbour, a lady. My sister come out to do the shopping. The lady see her. The lady run out. They fight. My nephews and nieces come out and help. My sister is lying on the ground, crying crying.'

'What was the fight about?'

He shrugs.

'Mans.'

'Do you punch anybody?'

'Course!' he says, laughing boyishly. 'I'm stay in the fale tonight?'

'No, you'll need to leave soon. I don't want anybody to know.'

'So beauty, the fale. You lucky, going sleeping here in your own fale. Just only you. You are free. All the boys are looking for your arse, but your arse is only mine. Why you are go for the walk every days? I'm go for the swim every days.'

'I don't know why I go for a walk every day. Why do you go for a swim every day?'

'So beauty, the swimming!'

Afterwards, I let him loll about in the bed a little more and then kick him out. Not so very long goes by before there's a quiet knock on my door.

'Already tucked up for the night?' says Guy.

'Yes, already tucked up, sweetheart.'

'Sweet dreams, darling.'

'You too, Guysie.'

I lie on my back under the net, in the darkness. My poor blameless old boy has guessed nothing, needless to say. A man so upright, so uptight, so whiter than white – well, how could he guess? Not long ago those same no-nonsense words were apt for me, too. Upright, uptight, whiter than white. Not now. I'm now – what?

Shillyshallying. Shifty.

Shady.

A fanfare of village roosters warns families that the sun is coming up. Lying back for a while, not thinking, I hear waves clucking, pigs oinking, children chattering, a gecko chittering. The gong sounds for breakfast. I duck into the shower, freshen myself quickly, scoot across the sand. Guy's waiting. He pecks me on my cheek. He takes me by the elbow. We trot up to the dining deck. We seat ourselves at a table near the water. Wavelets click against the deck posts. Gleams of low light, bouncing up from the lagoon, play across the beams and ceiling. Laauli, the very tall young man, begins serving us breakfast. He not only smiles warmly while doing so but even gives my poor old boy a pat on the shoulder, which is a kind thing to do.

'Laauli waits on table well, doesn't he?' says Guy.

'Mm?' I say distractedly, wishing we were being waited on by Karl. 'Yes, he's a nice lad.'

My mind keeps going over – over and over and over – what's been happening with Karl. I can't stop thinking about Karl. He makes me feel – unlike myself. Or more myself. Odd, the whole thing's so very odd. Here's me on one hand going through the motions of chatting with Guy – looking out at the lagoon, swatting the mosquitoes – yet all the time my body is going hot and cold, and giddy, and I can't stop thinking about those eyes, those hips – those lips. Oh my god, those lips! And those hands, so big and strong. And those legs, those feet, those big brown toes.

The tall boy comes back, still smiling.

'You like pancake and scramble eggs, Pru and Guy?'

'Yes, please,' I say. 'And would you fetch us a pot of coffee, Laauli?'

'Sweet,' he says, giving another little pat to Guy.

The day goes by in a very lively way, very happily, the two of us swimming, strolling, swimming, sunning ourselves, eating lunch on the deck, swimming. I don't snooze after eating. I'm too wakeful, too alert, too eagerly awaiting. Awaiting what comes about – comes about without my needing to do or say or even hint at anything – soon after we say goodnight. Karl comes whispering to my door. I open up. I let him inside. He does an even better job. Afterwards, I kiss him and kick him out.

Next morning I'm up once more with the birds. Once more I'm cavorting in the lagoon, diving and ducking and feeling so very alive, before getting even a first glimpse of Guy.

I float on my back under a rising sun, a flooding white light.

I feel good. I feel bad.

I feel good!

A week goes by, then a fortnight. I'm full of pep. Yet funnily enough, marvellously enough, even while my heart is pumping hard I seem able to stop almost at the drop of a hat and sit quite calmly, my muscles loosening, my eyes doing nothing but simply taking in what they see about them – the white sand, the blue lagoon, the green palms tossing in the breeze – and my brain seems to feel no need to think about any of it, of anything at all, really – all that seems to be needed is just to be here, where I am – heaven!

Guy behaves the same way.

'I feel as though till we came here my skull was stuffed full of wool,' he says after dinner one night.

'I feel as though my skull was just a hole,' I say.

'A hole?' he says, puzzled.

'A bolt hole – a hole that became spiderwebbed from waiting for me to bolt.'

The dear old boy has come to dinner wearing my violet and green lavalava. He found it on my fale matting earlier today. I'd dropped it, carelessly. He picked it up. He draped it around his hips. He looked at me warily. I looked back at him, also warily. I saw an awkward but peaceful travesty. A bony man with lined skin and thin lips and guarded eyes – guarded eyes peering at me intently – intently yet also with some curiosity.

A lined man whose thin lips slowly began grinning.

A man who began laughing.

He taps my hand, now – taps it very gently.

'Want to stay on, Pru?'

'Stay on?'

My heart begins bumping.

'I don't mean forever, necessarily. I only mean for now. I want to find out what might happen to me. I want to find out whether it means anything.'

'*It*, Guy?'

'You know – it, whatever it is – Samoa.'

My heart keeps bumping.

'Me too, Guy!'

His eyes shine under the starlight.

'You too, Pru?'

'I want to stay. I want to stay and – I mean – I'm already feeling so happy. I'm not sure whether what we're doing is good for us. I'm not sure of anything, really. I just know I want to stay. We could have a house built at Paradise in Heaven. We could have people lay out grounds. We could have people put in a swimming pool. We could – we could do anything!'

'I dare say we could, Pwu.'

'Let's then, Guysie. Let's go utterly and unashamedly *troppo*!'

CHAPTER FOURTEEN

'Well, beddy byes for me,' I say, after we've sat in close conclave for more than an hour plotting what to do with Paradise in Heaven.

'Right you are,' says Guy. 'I'll sit up a bit longer.'

A quick peck of a kiss.

My mind, of course, is on another kind of kissing. I can't get that kind of kissing out of my mind. Washing myself, brushing my hair, looking at my little travel clock, lying down in bed, trying to settle with a book, looking again at the clock, I think of nothing but Karl. The travel clock, needless to say, goes forward far too slowly. I try to think calming thoughts about water and greenery. I think instead about glossy curls, glossy lips, proud buttocks and – well, to be quite frank – cock. The heat of his cock. The softness, the strength, the slipperiness, of his cock.

I never really twigged about cock, till now.

'I feels good,' he said last night, after yawning. 'I wanna stay in the fale and more sex.'

'I want you to stay,' was my reply, 'but – '

He grinned at me.

'Sure, I know. I go home now.'

'I love you, Karl. I love you. I love you.'

He blew me a kiss before snatching up his lavalava – the green and turquoise lavalava worn by resort staff – shaking it out, wrapping it around his narrow waist and knotting it up. I watched closely. I always watch every one of his movements closely. And when not with him I'm thinking always about what he's doing, what he's thinking, what he's feeling. I'm lovelorn – I'm bewitched – I'm starstruck – I'm – I'm – forget about words! Our lack of a shared language can be a stumbling block, admittedly, but at the same time that very lack of language is perhaps why I've at last found a way to stop leaning on words, to stop thinking, and to start feeling.

I'm excited by my heart beating. I'm excited by being alive, by living. I'm excited by feeling that now is now, today is today.

Here, now.

Not yesterday, nor tomorrow.

I know now that to be yourself is to lose yourself. To be yourself is to be hit on the forehead by a kid biffing a stone, to bleat over a dropped lavalava, to ride a brown cock. To be yourself is to be nothing and everything – to be a mouth pressed against another mouth, a tongue lapping against another tongue.

To be yourself is not to be yourself.

Not to be is to be!

At last, when the travel clock has ticked and ticked too long for me to be able to stay still any more, I get out of bed, take a look in my silver travel mirror and see what I always see – grey hair, crowsfeet, turkey neck. Why on earth would a young man want even to look at, let alone fuck, this ageing woman? Well – he does. Karl does! I gaze adoringly at a pair of rubber jandals the lovely lad left behind last night.

I pick one up to give it a quick kiss.

Anyway, now that I'm out of bed there seems no point sitting inside, waiting, when the whisper of the waves and the wind in the palms call me outside. So, throwing on my dressing gown, I open the door and step on to the veranda.

Oops!

Guy, seated with a book on his own veranda only ten paces or so across the sand. He looks up. He meets my eye. Why is he awake? And he'll be asking himself why I'm still awake, too. Awkward. Karl will be here soon to give me my nightly rogering. Oh, it'd be just awful if my poor old boy were to find out about Karl. He'd be crushed if he knew about Karl.

'Still up, sweetheart?' I try.

'Yes, just enjoying the night sky, Pwu.'

'Mmm, beautiful isn't it? I couldn't get off to sleep so thought I might come out to feel the breeze.'

'Yes, er – '

He looks a bit fidgety. Oh dear, does he suspect something? Surely not. Of course not! Why would he suspect *me* of anything? Anyway, no time to think about that. I've only got time to think about how to get him off that veranda and behind his door and away to dreamland before the advent of a certain young man sporting curly locks. What can I do? I rack my brains. My brains, as you know, aren't the most rackable in the world, so really – well –

'Sweetheart, you mustn't stay up too late. You'll pay for it tomorrow if you don't get a good sleep.'

'I'll just count the stars for a bit. The stars will make me sleepy.'

'Why not turn in with your book?'

'No need to worry about me, Pwu. Actually aren't you the one who'd better tuck yourself up? You've been sleeping so little lately.'

No, no, no, this won't do at all! I've got to get out of here. I've got to track down Karl. I've got to head him off before –

'Guysie,' I say, trying hard to sound languid when really I'm now sweaty and palpitating, 'I may just go for a little stroll.'

'In your dressing down, Pwu?'

'Yes, it'll do.'

Guy looks at me almost with relief, oddly.

'Good idea, why not do that, darling?'

'Right ho!'

About to step down to the sand, I see out of the corner of my eye what I've been dreading. Karl under lamplight. Karl lightly lolloping across the sand with another young man, a very tall young man. Laauli. The two boys are whispering and giggling. They can't see me yet because my fale's in the dark. Nor can they see Guy. Laauli smacks Karl on the shoulder and runs away – away from Karl, but towards – damn, towards Guy. I signal swiftly to Karl – a signal telling him to keep walking.

Karl, being quickwitted, does keep walking.

'Malo, Pru,' he calls, cool as you please, scuffing across the sand. 'Malo Guy.'

'Malo, Karl,' calls Guy.

Laauli begins talking quietly to Guy. Only a few shakes of a lamb's tail are needed for me to bolt down my steps and on to the sand. I scurry off, walking at a right angle to the way taken by Karl. The night is dark, hot. Once out of sight of my poor old boy it's an easy trick for me to make a quick turn and track down the curly head of my lover bobbing about beneath a grove of coconut palms.

'Hey babe,' whispers the young man.

'Kiss me,' I say. 'Hard!'

He does what I say. He drives his tongue down deep. I grapple it with my own tongue. My hands are all over him, too, and his hands are soon all over me and it's not long before we're both panting.

'Let's back to the fale,' he says.

'Not just yet. We'll have to wait till Laauli has gone and Guy's no longer on his veranda. I don't want them to see us.'

Karl looks at me quizzically.

'Why?'

'Well, you know. I'd hate Guy to know what you and I are doing.'

Karl laughs out loud.

'Laauli already had nights with Guy. Lotsa nights. You don't know?'

What? What on earth does he mean? I can't quite grasp – it must be a cultural thing – one more of those endlessly odd things about Samoans.

'A lot of nights?' I try. 'A lot of nights with Guy?'

'Laauli horny with a hard dick.'

'Laauli – what?'

'He was kept fucking Guy. Lotsa nights. Why you look at me like that?'

What? How can it be – how can that be true? Karl's lying, obviously. Obviously he's pulling my leg. He's pulling my leg because if he's not pulling my leg then that would mean – would mean – well –

for heaven's sake, why would Guy want to have sex with a boy? Guy's a father, a husband. Why would he – ? It *can't* be true. Karl's got it wrong, quite clearly, he doesn't know what he's talking about – only – only – does this mean Guy – ?

Does this mean Guy's turning into Bertie?

No, there must be some mistake.

Guy doing the dirty on me, the deceitful bastard! How dare he? I mean – really! Yet perhaps, after all – well, perhaps it's just me? Perhaps it's just that he doesn't fancy me? I mean, nobody would point at me and say I was a sex kitten –

Oh, this is all ridiculous! Karl's got it wrong. Quite patently he's got it wrong.

I tell him so.

'You don't know for real?' he says.

'I know Guy, that's what I know. Who I know. Known each other our whole lives, Guy and I.'

Yet a few things are clicking into place suddenly. A lot of things! Click, click. Yes. Guy being gay would explain why he wasn't ever – keen – not too keen at all, really –

'I'll see you tomorrow,' I tell Karl.

'Eh?'

'Or perhaps not tomorrow.'

I'm striding across the sand, marching towards Guy. We need to have this out! A brisk breeze, blowing into my eyes from the ocean, has set the coconut palms thrashing. The stiff fronds seem to be shaking at me in fury saying, *go away white woman, go away*! Guy's fale. His lights are off. I'm storming up his steps. I'm knocking on his door. Rap rap! An ageing man edges open the door. A button has popped off his pyjama shirt. A few white curls of chest hair poke out of the gap. A white hank of his head hair sticks up like a steer's horn. He opens the door more widely.

I step inside, wondering what I'm about to say.

Guy switches on a lamp. The fale interior is orderly. A stack of books, squared off shipshape, sits atop a bedside cabinet. Woven mats on his floor have been aligned precisely to the north, east, south and west. Guy always occupies a space in an orderly way. Grey and fawn and brown shirts hang alongside brown and fawn and grey trousers and shorts. The only colour comes from my lavalava. The violet and lime green lavalava. It's hanging from a peg. It's lolling against the matting of the wall. Also there's a little flash of scarlet and yellow. Hibiscus. Scarlet blossoms opening out in the lamplight on a green twig. The twig pokes from a glass of water on the ledge of his window.

The fale is empty of any stray young man, thank goodness.

'Guy,' I say, surprised by how calm and friendly my voice comes out sounding. 'What's going on?'

Straightening his back, he looks me in the eye.

'Pru, we must talk. We must have a very serious talk.'

'What? What have you and that young man – what have you been doing?'

Guy looks braver than I think I've ever seen him before.

'Making love, Pru.'

Seating myself tidily on the end of his bed, my heart beating with a compelling sort of strong calmness, I know that what he and I are about to say to one another will mark the end of something – the end of something old – the start of something new. I don't know that I want to give up on the old. I don't know that I want something new. Or – is it only nonsense, what I'm thinking? I mean to say – it's everyone's story, isn't it – more or less everyone's, anyway.

A marriage. A long string of years. A straying.

A reckoning.

'Oh. I see,' I say. 'Yes, we need to have that talk.'

I do know, at least, that wherever we're going – the two of us – whether it's the two of us together or – or the two of us not together – golly, are we going to split up? What will people back home say? Mummy. Buffy! Anyway, what was I saying? Oh, yes – wherever we're going – and whether or not we want to go – I know now that somehow I've always known, yet didn't know I knew – you know, I knew about him, about me, about love, about life, about– well, about everything, really. Oh dear, it's not easy. I want to be happy. I want Guy to be happy. He wants to be happy. He knows I want him to be happy. He seats himself beside me, wrapped in his white dressing gown, and he begins speaking. He spills the beans. I help him out, when help is wanted, by prompting. We speak kindly.

'I worked it out myself, when I was twelve or so years old,' he says. 'I worked out that I was drawn to other boys.'

'Did you tell anybody?'

'Not a word. Not a hint of a word. You know me. I strangled every word. I had crushes on one or two boys at prep school. I never did anything. I never said anything. I had crushes on one or two boys at College. I never did anything. I never said anything. I had an awful crush on Clive when he and I were flatting together during our days at varsity.'

'Clive, you had a crush on Clive *Carrel*?' I say, poking my poor boy in the tummy.

'We got along pretty well, as you may recall. We talked about law and politics and history. He never knew I was mooning over his chin, his eyes, his body. At times, my longing for him was so intense I was almost paralysed – was able to do nothing other than sit alone, thinking about him, and trembling.'

'Clive's such a drip!'

'Love's blind, darling.'

'Love would need to be deaf to put up with Clive's pontificatings.'

'Yes, well, as I was saying, I never actually had the courage to say anything to him about my feelings, so it was just nothing but pontificating and being pontificated at about politics and history.'

'Sweetheart, you must have been so lonely.'

'You too, Pwu.'

Tears spring up in my eyes and begin trickling down my cheeks.

'Yes, I've been lonely, Guysie – *so* lonely – so *very* lonely.'

The words have come out without my knowing they were coming. I never knew how lonely I've been till now. We look at each other, appalled.

'Poor darling,' he whispers after a while.

'After all those years of mooning after boys, sweetheart, did you ever get around to actually – well, you know – doing anything with anybody?'

'No, nothing.'

I'm sobbing, now. I'm sobbing for him. I'm sobbing for me. We snuggle together more closely, saying nothing. The sobbing slows, after a bit. Guy gives me a pat.

'I did try to nerve myself into talking about it with you after we started our mariage blanc.'

Twenty years ago, in other words.

'Mariage blanc is an elegant way to say no fucking, Guy.'

He flinches, looks away, and then looks back at me, straight into my eyes. I'm sort of mewling, now – thinly, bitterly. His own eyes are filling up with tears, too.

'All right, darling,' I say quietly. 'Carry on with your story.'

'I've been working hard for years to stop myself from thinking about young men. I'm only drawn to young men. I don't know why. I've been working hard for years to stop myself from thinking about the whole thing. It's not been too tricky a task. After all, what young man worth his salt would want someone like me, someone so lacklustre, someone who never caught anyone's eye, someone now ageing, and ageing badly.'

'You're in pretty good shape, sweetheart.'

'I'm not, darling. I'm a stick. And the thought of being one of those wretched old men who drool over boys – well, the thought's been so loathsome that it made smothering my desires fairly easy. Actually, not really. It's been hard. One of the hardest things was thinking about you, Pru.'

'Me, Guy?'

'You, who've harnessed your own liveliness, your own cheerfulness, your own generous soul to someone so bloodless and dull and drab. It was hard enough when we were safely back home at Beauchamp. It's been harder since we came here to Samoa. It got very hard when I – well, when I started going with – er, started having sex with – '

He needs a bit of helping out.

'Laauli,' I say.

'Tui,' he says.

'What? *Tui*! Tui on Savai'i? What about Tui?'

'Tui more or less seduced me into – well, I won't spell it out, but he wanted sex. I couldn't believe what was happening. He took me down the beach a fair way from the villas. As you can imagine, it was almost overwhelming. I found it hard to believe he really wanted to be with me. We always went down the beach to the same spot.'

'A spot where the moonlight couldn't find you?'

'Yes, that's right.'

'A dark spot under a big palm where he'd pull you down onto the sand and fuck you?'

'Yes! What? I don't quite grasp how you – well, anyway, he seemed less keen on taking me to that spot after the first few nights. He stopped coming to get me from my villa. He stopped the – fucking. Very likely he got bored with being pawed by an old man.'

'Or had begun getting pawed by an old woman.'

Guy understands straightaway. He can be pretty quick on the uptake, can Guy. Oddly enough, I almost enjoy the way he looks suddenly bewildered, almost enjoy having a tale of my own to tell, and a tale that fits into his so snugly.

'God, straight from the husband to the wife?' he says. 'What a – '

'Scamp, shall we say?'

'Scamp will do. Thief, too. I gave him money. He told me some story – a load of cock and bull – about his mother being sick. He said she needed money to pay her medical costs.'

'How much did you give him, Guy?'

'Two hundred, Pru.'

'At least his rates were consistent. I paid him that, too.'

Guy looks at me, shocked. He shuts his eyes. I wonder if he's going to go back to crying.

He opens his eyes.

He looks at me almost merrily.

'Tui's a nice enough boy. I can understand why he'd try it on.'

'Yes. Droll that he rooked both of us. Droll that we're both such saps, you and I. It's not the same with Laauli, though, is it? He seems to be fond of you. D'you think Laauli has feelings for you – you know, serious feelings?'

Guy looks a little less merry.

'He's doing it because he's bored, I think. He says he finds village life very boring. How about your Karl? Does he have feelings for you, Pru?'

'No, he feels nothing.'

'Nothing?'

'Nothing. It's the same as with you and Laauli. Also – well, sweetheart, I've been paying him too.'

Guy lets out a little croak.

'Pru, I've been paying Laauli.'

I burst out laughing.

'Christ! I don't suppose one can blame them, can one, Guy? I mean to say – here we are, walking banks, at least in their eyes. And why, after all, would any young man be keen to – I won't say anything about you, but I'll certainly say it about myself – why the hell would any young man want to go with a hag like me in any other way than as a – not to put too fine a point on it – as a gigolo?'

'You're not a hag, Pru. You're pretty.'

'I'm an old hag and an old bag. How much have you been paying?'

'At first, nothing. He hinted at how hard up he was on our third – um – tryst. I gave him a hundred. We got into the habit of it. A hundred each time. And then a few days ago he hinted that perhaps I might be able to part with two hundred for each meeting. So, well – I decided to comply. How much have you been paying?'

'Hmm, well I'm afraid it's the same story. I was giving him a hundred every visit and then, just the other day, he asked for two hundred. Which is what I've subsequently been paying.'

'Oh. What day is it today, Pru?'

'Wednesday.'

'What day did he ask for two hundred?'

'Sunday.'

'Oh.'

'What day did Laauli ask for two hundred?'

'Sunday.'

'So they've been colluding to fix and then hike the pay rate. We've been a bit silly, haven't we, Guy? Are we just a couple of sleazy sex tourists, d'you think?'

'I rather think we are, darling.'

'Oh dear.'

'Quite.'

We have a consoling cup of tea, our first since breakfast. Guy, thank goodness, has a box of lapsang suchong. He always takes a travel teapot with him, together with a little spirit stove, so we're soon settled nicely. I pick up the hibiscus twig. I peer at its scarlet petals. I poke at one of its red scarlet pistils. I don't pluck one of the flowers. I don't tuck one behind my ear. I stick the twig back into its glass.

'I'm so bloody sick of this place, darling,' I say, picking up my tea and taking a grateful sip. 'Let's settle our bill at the front desk in the morning, go straight back to Apia, get the sand out of our hair, change our tickets for the first possible flight, and go home to Beauchamp.'

'Mm? It'll soon be spring, back home – spring in Canterbury!'

I think of early spring in Canterbury. White frosts in the first light of morning. Ice glittering on the peaks of Mount Hare. Warm norwesters making the mercury in the glass bolt skywards by midday. Snow melt surging down the Hare River. Birds mating, nesting. Our garden flowering.

'Yes, endless summer here in the tropics is wearying, isn't it?'

'And the daffodils will be out in a fortnight, Guy.'

'What's to be done about the property, Pru?'

'What property? Beauchamp?'

'Paradise in Heaven.'

'Oh, just give it to Stevenson. I don't want to come back here ever again.'

'Right you are, Pwu.'

I burst into more tears. He puts his arm around me.

'Can't believe what a fool I've been, Guysie. I've been so stupid. I want to go home. All these awful centipedes and geckos and stonefish and trigger fish and mosquitos and – these *people*! The people here just want to use us. I'm *longing* to go home.'

Part 3: CHAPTER FIFTEEN

An oval of old glass, very faintly greenish and slightly warped with age, shows me peering at myself severely. My face, as always, is too round. My hair, freshly cut in a new bob, is more or less all right. My makeup is near enough, at least for a drive around the district. My jacket and skirt, made for me from a soft bolt of light grey cashmere by the woman in town who does my tailoring, have been stitched seamlessly. The hoop earrings – simple, but gold – may be a mistake.

One more day.

Charcoal grey court shoes on my feet. My handbag is charcoal grey, too.

'I'm off, Guysie!' I call as I pass the door to his bedroom, where he's propped up reading poetry.

Verse is another of his hobby horses.

'Right you are, Pwu,' he croaks.

Trotting downstairs and then making my way through back of the house, I pop my head around the kitchen door to have a quick word with Tanya. I'm hoping she'll have the time to throw together something nice for pud this evening. A treat for Guy. The poor boy's been a bit under the weather for some days. Hence the croak. Nothing serious, only a head cold that's ended up working its way down to his chest.

'Sure thing, Pru,' she says in her pleasant contralto, obliging as always. 'I'll whip up an affogato for the two of you.'

'That'll tempt the patient's palate very nicely,' I say. 'Thanks so much, Tanya.'

'No worries. I can stay on an hour or so longer today.'

'You're a treasure!' I reply.

And she is, we're so lucky to have Tanya.

I take the Range Rover – I'm in the mood to ride high today – and soon am rolling down the driveway. An overcast day. Cold, even for early spring. I turn towards Hare Forest. Good pasture growth so far this spring in spite of the cold. The hedges want a good clipping. Now, let me see – what's on my list for today? Quite a lot. Jean, our old cook, has had a nasty fall and cracked her hip. I'll begin by popping in on her cottage in the township. A duty call, of course, and – well, a bit dreary. Afterwards, a meeting with Jayden and Buffy. The three of us have become a new vestry finances subcommittee and we'll need to toil for an hour or so over ways to try to cut parish administrative costs. Oh dear, more than a bit dreary. The reward will be lunch with Jim at Trecarrel. The reward won't be quite as enjoyable as one might wish, however, because Jim will want to pump me for all I'm worth about the meeting with Jayden and Buffy.

As always, paddocks stretching away.

As always, plantations strutting in point-blank rows.

We've been back home for more than a fortnight now. At first it seemed mostly to be a matter of sleeping. Also a matter of coping with our voicemail. Well, my voicemail really. Guy seldom gets calls. My phone was choked with a horrible backlog.

'Mummy, what's going on? Are you so besotted with sun and surf you've lost the faculty of speech?'

'Ma? Pops? Call me!'

'Pru? Need your thoughts on the *latest* gambit by bloody *Buffy*!'

'Mummy, why the hell aren't you answering?'

'Pops, Ma, guessing you'll have heard about Kwok and Kwok going under the receivers? No need to worry. You won't lose a lot. Will keep you both in the loop. Cheers!'

'Mummy, you're still not answering. What are you two doing? Are you, like, lost on some desert island or something?'

'Pru! *Frightful* row at the vestry!'

The phone rings again now. Charley. Not good, given that it's late in the evening on her side of the world and very likely she's been drinking.

'Hi darling,' I say, holding the phone with one hand while using the other hand for steering, which is a bit naughty, against the law, I think.

'Mummy, I've been mulling over my childhood days.'

'Have you sweetheart?'

'Yes. I've begun going to a psychotherapist. Did I tell you? No? Well, I am. Questions are coming up. Mummy, remember how you used to call us the offs? Tim and me. I've never told you till now but – well, I always felt a bit – hurt – about that. I mean, I know you thought it was a joke, very funny, most amusing, haha, but – well, it was pretty wounding – and it was the same for Tim, too, probably – well, I can't speak for Tim – I hardly ever knew Tim and I know him even less, now, I mean – he never phones, and he's always so busy making money over there in Honkers, and – you know, sometimes I feel crap, Mummy. I feel really crap, sometimes, Mummy.'

'Do you, darling? Oh, poor old you. A thing with some young chap gone a bit wrong?'

'No. No, it's – well it's about you, really.'

'Me, sweetheart?'

'Do you love me, Mummy?'

'Darling, we both love both of you.'

The poor tipsy child starts gabbling, very quickly.

'Mummy, you don't seem to get the fucking point. I don't want you to use the first person fucking plural. I don't want you to fucking speak as though you and Papa are some fucking sort of corporate fucking entity. I don't want you to speak as though Tim and I are some fucking sort of corporate entity. I mean, for fuck's sake, do you love me?'

'Look here, sweetheart, have you – well, darling, have you been drinking?'

Charley lets out a hard little laugh.

'Drinking? No. I'm not drunk, Mummy. It's not fucking booze that's making me so fucking unhappy.'

I've had enough of this hectoring.

'Oh for heaven's sake, grow up Charley.'

'And you – you just – *fuck* yourself, you fucking – fucking cow!'

The phone goes dead.

Yes, well perhaps I didn't quite handle that so very tactfully. All the same, need she swear like a shearer? Also, the whining! One thing to be feeling low. Quite another thing to – well, to wallow. The more one wallows the more one sinks. She's got everything going for her, hasn't she? After all, I mean to say, nine out of ten girls would crawl over broken glass to have so little that's wrong with their lives and so much that's right.

Wouldn't they?

'Yin Yang needs a kick up the bum,' says Jim, red and sweaty and happy from a morning with her young bay gelding. 'Been trying to get the cheeky bugger ready for dressage.'

I never understood why Jim gave the bay a name so outlandish – well, outlandish for Jim – as Yin Yang.

'He's not keen to do what he's told?'

'He's keen to do what he's told *when* he's keen to do what he's told. Took him out for a play in the top paddock at the start of the week. Not too bad. A tootle along the road yesterday. He's in fine fettle but tense as a coiled spring and he bloody well kept swinging his head about and bucking. Pru, how's your health? You're not looking too flash lately.'

'Perfectly fine, Jim. Well, oversleeping – but you know me, oversleeping is standard. Apropos sleeping, last night I had the funniest nightmare about the spring fete and you and Buffy. You were a horse, Jim.'

'*Was* I indeed?'

'An exhibition draught horse. You kept kicking Buffy.'

'Well that sounds satisfying.'

'Your hooves were fitted with machetes instead of horseshoes.'

'Oh.'

'Quite. A lot of blood. Chop, chop, chop!'

Jim looks at me askance, clearly worrying, but then quite as clearly making up her mind to let it go.

'Right you are, Pru. Anyway, this morning, thought I'd do some canter-trot transitions with Yin Yang, but the cheeky bastard had other plans. Speed, mostly. He went from slow as a sloth one minute to next minute bouncing on the spot and tearing off.'

'Were you using the whip?'

'Only the schooling whip. No good. Just made him buck. Dropped it, took off my spurs and gave gentleness a go. A lot of begging and buggering round and then in the end I did get him to walk, trot and canter straight when I wanted him going straight, and in a circle when I wanted him circling.'

Keen myself to take a hack over our paddocks, I change into riding togs upon getting back home to Beauchamp. On my way out of my room I pop my head in to say hello to Guy.

'Slept at all, sweetheart?' I ask.

'Not a lot, darling,' he says. 'I'm doing a lot of lying awake, lately – actually I lie awake for hours every night.'

'We need to do a bit of a swap, don't we? You need some of my sleep and I need some of your wakefulness.'

'I cry. Do you cry, Pwu?'

'I do, Guysie.'

'I lie in bed on my side and tears roll from my eyes and trickle across the thin skin of my temple and drip into my ear.'

'Can tears, if enough of them fill an ear, cause death by drowning?'

'I'm inclined to hope so.'

We laugh, a bit bitterly but very companionably.

Bob, my biddable chestnut, happily lets me saddle him up. The dear old boy was pleased to see me when I first walked towards him with a saddle a fortnight ago. He's always pleased to see me after I've been away on holiday. Today he's nice and loose on the buckle, the way he's nearly always nice and loose on the buckle when we go for a wander over the property. His withers swell and sink, swell and sink, the ribcage hardly seeming to move between my legs. Hooves tidily clip the gravel of the riding track.

Not only does know his way, he knows my ways. And, lucky chap, he knows what it is to be alive. He and every other horse, and every dog, every sheep, every bird, knows without knowing.

I, on the other hand –

Songbirds on all sides are piping.

I'm feeling all right. Well, near enough anyway. Here, now.

Silly of me to think that answers of some sort might be found simply by mooning around under palm trees and letting myself go in for a little overdue lovemaking. No answers there for the finding. To be yourself means nothing, really, it's only a question of getting on with things, handling things as well as you can handle things, no matter what comes up – or doesn't come up – and then, what comes up next, and so on, and then – well, getting on with dying.

A mouth pressed against another mouth – a tongue lapping against another tongue.

You've got no self to be, really.

To be is nothing.

The day may be cold but anyone with half an eye can see how spring has begun drawing new life up from the quiet thin earth of Canterbury. Our grounds are a froth of fresh greenery. Twiggy nests in the treetops are crammed with cheeping chicks. The sky's alive with honeybees, bumblebees, beetles, flies, whirring and buzzing and clicking. Willows, poplars and birches have leafed fully. Oaks, sycamores, beeches and plane trees are leafing now. Ashes and walnuts will leaf later to complete the canopy.

We amble into the woodland.

I look up through the boughs at the blank grey sky. A harrier hawk, an old fellow, wheels sideways while making a courting cry. Short shrieks, starting high then falling away. A hen hawk gives her reply. She sounds a lot younger than the cock hawk yet seems serious about courtship.

Shove my feelings down – that's the only way.

Bob, on the bit, wanders out of the woodland and into the wether paddock.

'Samoa,' I say to myself.

Bob blows suddenly. A shiver runs through his body. What has he seen or felt? I look about, peering east, north, west and seeing nothing. The paddock. Wethers chewing grass. A row of cypress. A wink of water glimpsed between willows.

He does see ghosts sometimes, does Bob.

A pat or two, a soothing word or two, and off he ambles, his carriage good. Bob's carriage is always good. He's a good boy. The hawk swoops north towards Mount Hare. I know him well, that hawk. All year round he gets his living from our land. After his courtship of the hen a handful of eggs will be laid in some sheltered spot among long grasses on the banks of the Hare River. Bob ambles through the wether paddock. Sheepish heads lift wary eyes, peering at us through little oblong pupils. One or two wethers call or cry. Afterwards the mob looks down once more and gets on with the dogged cropping of clover and grass.

I feel sorry for wethers.

Two fencers are at work along the boundary. Bob, guided by my movements, ambles over to them for the sake of country courtesy. The boss fencer is squat, square and moves slowly. A greasy beanie, knitted by his wife from coarse grey wool, hugs his skull. His cheeks are red and raw. The offsider, a young fellow of twenty, sports a shock of black hair and moves lithely. The work of stringing has heated him up, in spite of the cold grey sky, so he's stripped down to a white singlet. He's a young Maori. The hair on top of his head is glossy, wavy. Inside his armpits, it's glossy, curly. Nipples prick against the taut white cotton of his singlet.

I feel a sting in my own nipples – and then a stab between my legs.

'Nice work, well done,' I say, nodding.

'Cheers,' says the boss fencer, looking up, nodding back, not wasting words.

Workmen in the country seldom waste words. The offsider, behaving in neither a friendly nor unfriendly way, tests the tension in some newly strung wire. Overhead, the hawk is still wheeling.

Bob, taking my tip, ambles off once more towards the Hare River.

A pine plantation, marching to the east, marks the divide between our paddocks and those belonging to the Craigs. A hardworking, straightforward family, the Craigs. They farm a couple of hundred hectares cut out from Beauchamp around a century ago. Not our sort of people, needless to say. They stick to their own kind, send their kids to the state school in the township and do nothing for show. Our nearest neighbours, in one sense, the Craigs. Yet in another sense they live far away.

I can hear the odd moo from beyond the cypress rows. The Craigs, like lots of others these days, are going in for dairying.

Cows – on the dry plains of Canterbury!

My phone rings.

'Mummy, one or two more things to say – '

Oh dear.

'Yes, Charley?'

'My psychotherapist has been asking how I ended up getting anorexic during my days as a schoolgirl.'

Charley followed in my footsteps when it came to schooling. We boarded her out as soon as she was ready. You know, when she was seven years old. Primary school years at Selwyn House. High school years at St Margaret's. She needed the companionship. A country homestead can be quite lonely. Tim was a boy, so he was no company. He was away at boarding school anyway. No other children lived closer than a couple of kilometres away. Well, our shepherd, living in the cottage behind the sheds, was a married man and he and his wife had three boys. Lively young scraps who floated sticks down the water races and whooped around outside the cottage. Our forester had two girls. He and his wife were in the other cottage, by the gateway. Very nice youngsters, those girls and boys. Hearts of gold.

Not, of course – well, not in the stud book, shall we say?

'Anorexic, sweetheart? You weren't anorexic. You were just a fussy eater.'

'I wasn't a fussy eater, Mummy. I was a wretched little slip of shit and thought the only way anyone would ever come to love me would be if I made myself pretty.'

'Charley, why dwell on the past, sweetheart? We could all blame the past – couldn't we – for our troubles today?'

She did struggle a bit after we sent her away. When we dropped her off at Selwyn she got quite upset and there was rather a scene. Very difficult for everybody. I felt badly about it but reminded myself that she'd soon get settled, get into the swim, the way I did during my school days. I knew it was best for her to be boarding. And soon, during the hols, she was getting gaggles of girls to come from school and stay. Or she was off to their places with her tennis racquet and her riding gear. She was Miss Popularity.

'Charley, darling, you're becoming a bit of a bore about this, quite frankly.'

'And you're being an absolute mare. You've spent your whole life since you whelped me from that womb of yours palming me off on other people. You need to know that being your daughter hasn't been very cool, basically.'

What am I feeling?

Hurt, shocked, guilty, angry.

'Well do make up your mind where you want to yard me, darling,' I say. 'You called me a mare just now, but you said I was a cow this morning.'

'You're neither. You're a bitch.'

The phone, once more, goes dead.

Bob, on the bit, comes to the Hare River.

'Good boy,' I murmur, with no particular intent.

A gelding, ten years old, he's a big lad, my Bob. He stands at a little over eighteen hands. Yet he picks his way daintily down a winding pathway under soft green willows till we come out on the white shingle bed of the Hare River. A shingle bed bushed, tufted, spiked, with grasses and shrubs. Gorse. Broom. Silver tussock. Braided streams, twittering, turn and twist their way through the shingle banks. Wrybills are at work. Terns, too. And banded dotterels. And black-billed gulls. A mullein has begun bolting from its silvery woollen muff. A briar rose holds out an offering of sour little flowers. I picked rose hips, when I was a girl, for the sake of biting into their shining sourness. I picked them on days when I found myself wandering alone, which was most days. Cow parsley has started to flower in the warmest spots. As a girl I would sometimes pull up a cow parsley and gnaw its foot, its little parsnip.

I look up at Mount Hare.

A high heap of dark indigo, the shape of a cast sheep. I've been looking at Mount Hare all my life, more or less. I looked at the northeastern flank when growing up at Saxon Downs. I look at the southeastern flank now I'm a grown woman here at Beauchamp. Mount Hare, always there, hunched high under an always shifting sky.

Yes, always there, Mount Hare.

Yesterday – tomorrow.

I know what will come tomorrow. The monthly meeting of the horticulture committee of the West Canterbury Agricultural and Pastoral Association. I'm chairing. The day after tomorrow, the vestry. Two days after tomorrow, the committee of the Worthington Youth Cancer Foundation.

No rest for the wicked.

A smiling young brown man stripping off a lavalava –

Tomorrow – I know what will come tomorrow, and the day after tomorrow –

Tears flowing, snot streaming from my nostrils, I think about the years waiting for me at the end of this year, and then the year after next year, and – and me doing nothing, nothing but keeping busy, nothing but sticking to ways I've always stuck to, nothing but doing things I was taught were the right things in what I was told was the right way, year after year, spring, summer, autumn, winter – paddocks fresh and green, then sere and yellow, then red and brown and gold, then white with frost or snow. The earth swinging in space mindlessly. The easterlies blowing brisk off the Pacific. The norwesters blowing hot off the Alps. The southerlies blowing cold from the Pole.

And me dying, a lifeless end to a life not lived.

I'm not as brave as Bertie Blandwood.

No young man is ever going to curl up with me, supple and musky, looking at me with big brown eyes. The stable door of my life has been locked tight. And was there ever anyone inside to bolt? Guy loves me as best he can, of course, and I love him as best I can, but he's given up hope. I've seen it happening since we got back. He's shutting up shop. Actually, what do we want, the two of us? Love? Or heat? All we want, I think, is some young man urgent and hard and hot and holding us, at least for a short while – knowing, or kidding ourselves that we know, our sad old carcasses are not only wanted but grasped, gripped, groped, probed, filled with flowing life.

A flock of finches, bright red and soft violet, flashes by.

Again my phone rings.

'Pru, not good news,' croaks Guy. 'Come up to the house?'

I feel sick. I don't want to know bad news. I don't think I can cope with bad news. I'm too weary. I'm wearied by going on living.

'A death, darling?'

'No, it's – it's a disappearance.'

'I'm down at the river. Tell me the story now.'

'It's Tim. The police are chasing him. He's run away from Hong Kong. They think he's somewhere in Thailand. They've got a warrant to arrest him for fraud and embezzlement. He must have been tipped off about the warrant. He flew to Bangkok. He got a cab at the airport there and since then no sightings. What should we do?'

'We've done it already.'

'What?'

'We made him who he is. Coldhearted. Conscienceless.'

'Well done, darling, for summing it up so concisely. Apparently a lot of his money losses were to do with drugs.'

'Christ.'

'He's an addict, or so the police say.'

'Guy, while we're getting stuck in and blaming ourselves, we should say something about Charley. We made her who she is, too.'

'Who is she, Pru?'

'Vain. Shallow. Unhappy. And an anorexic alcoholic.'

'Phew, you're not wanting to mince words today, are you, darling?'

'The road of our lives is paved with minced words, sweetheart. We've fucked over the offs and ourselves right royally.'

'And now we may be penniless, too.'

'We deserve everything we get.'

'We do, Pwu.'

CHAPTER SIXTEEN

'The shady avenue gliding, um, sinuously through the fresh green fields and leafy spring woodlands of, er, the magnificent but welcoming historic homestead,' I tell my phone while my wee car farts its way into yet another snooty country estate, 'take you back in a blink, um, a wink, one hundred years to the setting of some gorgeous garden party in a story by Katherine Mansfield.'

A norwester is blowing.

It's hot, bloody hot. A stark, blustery blue sky.

No need to korero with my phone, really. Only doing it to keep my hand in. The boss has sent me to this wedding not to write it up but just to take pics. Our pro photographer is busy with a bigger job. All we need, says the boss, are standard line-ups of dowagers and other rich wrinklies hiding their crepey skin under the brims of picture hats, along with their braying broods of smug youngsters, mug shots of the whole loaded lot under the eaves of sweeping verandas or the heaving boughs of trees on sweeping greenswards, line-ups of costumed and bejewelled and hatted but somehow dowdy nobs belonging to Ye Olde Canterbury Stuffed and Mounted Brigade.

'Can't we just use some of the pics we shot at one of those weddings a year or two ago?' I said to the boss. 'The pics are always the same – ropes of pearls and rows of horsey teeth.'

'Nice try,' she said.

'Soz, boss.'

I was wanting to get out of the job because, to be honest, I'm more than over these people. They're always courteous to me, so courteous you could easily kid yourself into thinking they're decent people. Well, most of them do happen to be more or less decent, but when you get yourself mixed up with this creditworthy crew you need to keep telling yourself they have no idea how the world works, the real world, how it works, or more often doesn't work, for nearly everyone they don't know and won't ever get to know.

Mum died a fortnight ago.

Maybe the next step is back to Mexico?

I swing into a parking paddock. I slot myself into a tight spot between a massive Lexus and a mighty Mercedes-Benz.

'You'll be Dwayne?' honks a hearty man about my age who nabs me after I've walked through an oak wood to the party.

'Yip.'

'Miles Lambert,' he honks on, grabbing my hand and giving it a plunge or two in his big red paw. 'Make yourself at home – my wife over there, in the cream lace, if you need any tips.'

'Ta.'

The Ridges is a sheep station belonging to Miles and Elizabeth Lambert. Miles got it from his father, also called Miles, who got it from his father, Marmaduke, blah blah blah. Lawns have been mown and rolled and raked between a dark artificial lake and a smart groomed hillock. All three floors of the house – a huge hulk built in the late nineteenth century, Queen Anne – are jumbled up and down with gables and dormers and bay windows and bulging porches and bulbous columns, the whole lot topped with heavy terracotta tiling. Chimneystacks, jutting from the roofs, look like watchtowers where wool lords could post shepherd sharpshooters to keep a lookout for stray mobs of lost sheep and herds of two-legged hoi polloi.

Hoi polloi like moi.

Fuck, I'm feeling totally rinsed by having to put up with this crap, all these braying inbreds.

Men in morning suits. Women in dresses and hats. Sky blue and grass green and cherry red and canary yellow. High heels spiking the turf. Bling, but classy bling. The tinkle of champagne flutes. A string orchestra playing light classics. Waiters serving hors d'oeuvre from silver trays. Guests eddying, drinking, talking, drinking. I do my own eddying, eyeing things up, listening to what people are saying.

'Spot of trouble with the youngest of the fellows in the steer paddock – '

'Youngest of the stockmen?'

'Youngest of the steers.'

I keep eddying.

'An antique shop tucked away off Chester Street West. You must go and have a bit of a poke about. Just mention my name. He keeps a lot of the best stuff out the back. You absolutely must go and have a poke about.'

'Any plans for Carnival Week?'

'Just the races, this year. And we'll do the hunt club ball. And there's the odd dinner party.'

I take pics, lots of pics, most of which will end up in the bin back at the mag cause we can only run half a dozen or so from this wedding. After snapping each pic I go through the routine of writing down people's names for the captions below the shots. The names are nearly always names I've heard before, cause there's only so many names among this crowd. After twenty minutes or so I'm gaping with boredom while hanging around a group near the ornamental fountain. A group talking about the local body elections held a couple weeks ago.

'The polling in Christchurch went well enough. Reds didn't get the mayoralty.'

'Wish we could say the same about Worthington.'

Worthington's this district. The electors threw out the old mayor – a property developer – and voted in a human rights lawyer.

'Heard the speech she gave at Hare Forest. Could hardly credit what she was saying. Social justice this! Social justice that! Nagging harridan whose people were perfectly good sorts, salt of the earth types. Father a farm labourer, hard worker, kept his nose clean. Mother on checkout at the supermarket, though when banging about the saucepans in her kitchen perhaps a bit too fond of the cooking sherry.'

'At least she cooked! More than can be said of so many of those working mothers these days, bringing up their kids on takeaways.'

'Quite. Anyway, evidently our admirable new mayor went off the rails when she was a teenager and got herself pregnant by some drugged-up bloody oik of a no-hoper then sponged off the taxpayer as a solo mother till she somehow managed to sleepwalk her way into a law degree and now wants to make the district inclusive and multicultural, for god's sake!'

A round of grunts shows that everyone in the group agrees wholeheartedly. I step forward, simpering, and ask them to bare their fangs for a pic. After the baring I get them to spell out their names in case the pic makes the cut. Hester Carrington. William Locke-Luxmoore. Lucy Locke-Luxmoore. Gerald Fyffe. Caroline Tancred.

'Tancred? You'll be related to, like, Pru Blandwood? She's a Tancred, right?'

'Cousins. Why?'

'We did a story about Beauchamp.'

'Did you? She's here somewhere, and so's Guy.'

Not too long afterwards I find Guy and Pru whispering to one another under a big cypress. Pru, looking pretty tasty, wears a pink silk suit and a choker of pearls round her neck. Guy, on the other hand, looks – well, random. How come I didn't notice him in the crowd till now? Above the waist he looks like all the other guys – morning suit – but below the waist instead of pants he's sporting a lavalava. A violet lavalava spotted all over with big green flowers, not only wrong for this sort of wedding but cheap, too. Shabby.

'Heya,' I say. 'You into things Pasifika, Guy?'

He looks me over, works out who I am and holds up his hand for me to shake.

'Afternoon,' he says. 'Not so much into things Pasifika as no longer into wearing full morning suit.'

'Yeah? How come?'

'A very long story, Wayne,' cuts in Pru. 'A short answer would be that over the winter we went a troppo in Samoa.'

'Dwayne. Cool.'

'Not cool, steamy. At the end of our trip I binned this ratty scrap of a lavalava but my wayward husband, while I wasn't looking, salvaged it and hid it in his suitcase. Apparently he'd made up his mind that though he was no longer troppo he'd like something to help him think about the late Bertie. And today he thought he'd like the late Bertie to be here with the rest of the family.'

'Yeah?'

Who the fuck's the late Bertie? And what the fuck does he have to do with a lavalava? Obviously it's meant to be funny in some secret sort of way.

Guy starts laughing. A sad sort of laughing.

'I wasn't brave enough to roust out some henna, mind you,' he says, 'to do full honour to Bertie's memory.'

Pru laughs now, too. Hoot hoot hoot.

Yip, complicated private joke, obviously.

'Okay if I take a pic? The lavalava will look good in my mag.'

'We'd rather not,' says Pru. 'Lovely to see you again but now we're off for a little stroll.'

Squelch.

I let myself take one quick look at those nice tits of hers before she turns on her heels. A subtext or two in what she was saying, but fucked if I can guess any of those subtexts. And now I better get on with my job. A couple of young matrons nearby, pearled up, legs golden from winter holidays, hips swathed in tight couture miniskirts. The two of them, wasted on the champagne, seem to be talking about their husbands.

'Oh, but Rupert can't *bear* that! He always likes me to – '

'Well, isn't that *peculiar*! Mike just loves – '

'God, I'm feeling sick – between you and me I could seriously throw up all over the hors d'oeuvres.'

A while later I find myself wandering through a clipped shrubbery. Green, shady. Cool and nice after the glare of the lawns. Coming to a corner, turning it, I catch sight of a blur of soft pink. Pru, in her silk, standing behind a high lemonwood hedge. She's peeking through a topiary diamond cut into the flank of the lemonwood. The diamond allows her to see the people on the lawns. Pru can see them but they can't see her because the diamond is too narrow.

'Sick of the freak show, Pru?'

Starting, she steps back before looking me up and down quite coolly.

'You're a bit cruder now than when you came to our place last autumn, Dwayne.'

'Cruder? Or, like, more real?'

'Do crude people think they're more real?'

'Dunno. What's real?'

'Not me, for one. You?'

We eye each other up.

'Money's real,' I try. All the money here, like, all the old money.'

'Money's not real,' says Pru.

'Fuck sake. This crowd here is just, like – you know! All that crowd out on those lawns listening to that string fucking orchestra. Well, scratch that. Not listening to that string fucking orchestra cause the only sounds they really hear are the sounds of themselves gossiping about each other and slagging off anybody like me. You know, anybody who so totally looks like what I am, bogan-dressed-up-to-look-like-dressed-up-bogan. Fuck it, it's crap. I mean, for fuck sake look at Elizabeth Lambert!'

'Elizabeth Lambert?'

She peeks again through the topiary.

'Oh, you mean Buffy – everyone calls her Buffy.'

'Yeah? *Everyone* does, do they? Okay, so your Buffy bug-eyed bloody Lambert wearing that, like, cylinder of off-white lace. And those mother-of-pearl buttons all over it like a rash. And then on top of her smirking grimacing that kind of squashed top hat, with all those lashings of off-white lace, and those off-white silk roses, and that big brooch of gold and pearls and ivory, and those three strings of off-white pearls around her stringy vermilion neck. Well, ask me what I reckon and I'd say she looks like a wired Persian cat.'

'I wouldn't say a Persian cat. I'd say a fat ferret.'

'Yeah that'll do too.'

'What's *wired*?'

'Wired. On the pipe. You know, amped by a couple pipes of meth.'

'Meth?'

'Methamphetamine.'

'Forager's gin more likely, Dwayne.'

'What? Anyway, the look in everyone's eyes, everyone here, everyone's eyes are sort of mad. I don't think they understand how mad it is, what they're doing and saying and wearing and thinking.'

She's smiling. She looks away. She looks back and –

Fuck!

Defo, this time, the squiress has defo been checking out my tackle!

I take one more wee peek at her sweet tits.

'Well, to be fair to my friends and neighbours and family on the other side of this peephole,' she says, sort of drawling, 'everyone everywhere when ganged up together goes a bit mad.'

She smiles at me calmly.

I let out a laugh.

'Yeah, the special madness of your gang isn't a madness I seem to like a lot, is all.'

At the same time, I'm liking the way the age lines round her nice eyes and her nervous mouth are creasing upwards, making her look somehow weary. Weary of living? Yet still, somehow, hoping. And dreaming? As though she's still young, still a girl, still a blameless little kid.

'Well to be perfectly frank, nor am I sure I like it myself. Jury out on whether I like you, Dwayne.'

'Hah!'

'You're a quickwitted chap.'

'You're a lovely lady, Pru. And you're sexy.'

Stepping forward, guessing now that she wants what I want, I plant a quick kiss on her lips. A quick dry kiss. A gallant sort of kiss. The kiss of a courteous cavalier who wants to salute a lady with his lips while letting her know he knows she's way above him, unless, unless the lady should happen to fancy a quick shag?

The squiress steps back.

'We won't, Dwayne.'

'You liked the kiss. I can tell. You'd like to keep kissing.'

I'm not wrong. She steps forward. And soon we're at it like knives in a sort of box room behind the stables. Pru's not shy. True she's got a couple of love handles spilling out over the top of her pure white knickers, before I pull those knickers down her soft cushiony thighs. But, like they say, something to get a grip on. Riding gear is lying about on the floor, getting underfoot, along with old polo mallets.

'Hmm, so that's what one calls manscaping?' she says, having unpeeled my jeans and tugged down my jocks.

'Yip. You like?'

'Puts me in mind of a lawn mown a good deal too close.'

As for her – wow! She's not so much a lawn as a thicket. Obviously doesn't shave or wax or clip or anything. And, getting my face down there, getting a closer eyeball, I see it's more even than a thicket, more even than a bush, it's a native forest, dark and tangled. And wet! I go in for a good whiff, properly snorgle her pussy. Lush! A rich musky scent. Sweaty. Yummy! Deep inside the salty darkness two little lips are peeping out. Peeping out, nestled, pink and glistening. You could call one coral and the other, not quite the same shade, maybe you could say rose. Two cute little lips just puckering at me, so down goes my tongue! And soon my whole head has buried itself in her native forest, my nose snuffling up all the scents, my tongue licking and tickling and probing those pink lips.

Paradise!

Afterwards, she starts to cry.

No gulps or sobs, just a quiet sort of trickling. I look out a little square window and see the branches of a cedar shaking in the norwester, trembling nervelessly. A blackbird is jerking its head up and down, poking its way through a bed of leaf litter beneath the cedar, yanking out worms, or slugs. Pru keeps trickling. I don't know what to do. I pat her for a while, just the safe spots, the bland bits, avoiding tits, bush, clit. And soon I get the sense that her crying is sort of okay, okay with her, I mean, or at least not my fault, not me having done anything wrong.

'I've been weeping a fair bit lately,' she says, sitting up suddenly. 'Guy, too.'

'Sweet,' is the wittiest thing I can think of saying.

'You're a nice enough fellow. No, you're a nice fellow. No caveats. I don't know if it's good manners or not to say so, given how touchy people can be about this sort of thing these days, but you're my first ever Maori.'

'Yeah?'

'Only you'd better get your clothes on and get back to the wedding.'

'Right. Okay.'

I feel like a kid whose mum has just told him to get on with his homework. I'm standing up, have

begun following her orders, and now she pecks a kiss
on one of my bum cheeks.

'A very nice fellow,' she says graciously.

'You're a lovely lady, Pru,' I say, which is lame
given that I've said it already. 'This wedding sucks,
so I'm going to dip.'

'Dip?' says Pru. 'Go for a swim?'

'Go,' I say,

'Good. Lucky you. I've got to stay.'

Grabbing up my gear, I blunder away.

Weird, or what?

CHAPTER SEVENTEEN

I stop for a bit to look at a bank of primroses in a shady spot. All my life I've seen primroses bloom like lost promises every spring. I've seen them blooming under the canopy of the big trees at Saxon Downs. I've seen them blooming at Selwyn House. I've seen them blooming at St Margarets. I've seen them blooming at Whitepark. And, for more years than I care to think about, I've seen them blooming here at Beauchamp. Primroses are no longer flowering elsewhere in the grounds, since we're getting well on in the season, but in this spot, where the soil is very cool, they come in late and are now thriving.

Stooping, I snuff up the light fragrance.

Flowery.

Stooping some more, I pick one blossom and lift it to the light to look at it closely. Soft – white – opening out into a pretty yellow heart. Lifting it higher, I stick it behind my ear and take one last look at the whole flowery bank.

I think of hibiscus.

Scarlet petals, floppy. Scarlet pistil, stiff.

I turn away. I set off along the poplar avenue towards the hexagon and its ornamental urn.

I don't know whether to say yes or no.

Guy and I had a serious conference under a cypress at that tiresome wedding yesterday. We talked about why. We talked about why not. We made up our minds that we'd give ourselves twenty-four hours to make up our minds. We no sooner agreed to that timetable than we were bailed up by Dwayne.

Dwayne –

I feel myself smiling.

I'd love to know what Buffy would say if she knew what happened in the harness and tackle room at The Ridges.

Anyway, only an hour or so from now my mind has to have been made up. And my old boy's mind has to have been made up. I'm taking a wander through the grounds doing my best to work everything out. So much has been happening. Charley gone into rehab. Tim found and arrested in Yangon. The news came when we were crunching our way through toast and sipping coffee at breakfast this morning.

'Yangon?' I asked Guy. 'Where's that – it's not Thailand, is it?'

'Myanmar.'

'Myan – what?'

'Myanmar. You know, darling. Burma.'

'Oh god, the prisons there must be appalling!'

'They'll shunt him back to Hong Kong, I dare say.'

'I don't think I'd care to spend many nights in a Hong Kong prison either, sweetheart.'

Kwok and Kwok have indeed gone broke but what's owned by, or owed to, the company turns out to be worth nearly as much as what's owing. Although we'll make a loss it won't be too bad. A million or two. Lots left in the kitty. Tim seems to have been so unhandy at cooking the books that he wasn't able to get away with a hefty sum even when doing his very best at embezzling.

Anyway, now I've come to the hexagon and I'm looking back at the house and somehow I seem to have made up my mind. The windows of the house are gleaming in the slowly lowering light of the sun, a yellowish sun westering its way towards the Alps. All the birds seem to be singing.

The globe sits on top of the loo table, as always, at one end of the library. The two sofas, their oxblood red leather buttoned down tightly, flank the table on either side, as always. A lovely light floods the room from the twinned set of french windows. Guy stands, quiet and bony, wearing the lavalava, by the globe.

'Yes or no, Pwu?'

'Yes. You?'

'Yes.'

'Gosh – right!'

He begins spinning the old globe, once more playing that game he often plays. Only this time my task is to close my eyes until it stops spinning. And it's not a game we're playing. Or is it? My eyes closed, I wait for the word from Guy. I can hear, while I wait, a tiny trilling of little brass cogs. The trilling slows. The trilling stops.

'Now,' says Guy.

I reach out with my right index finger – my eyes still closed – touch the globe and then open my eyes to see upon which spot I've planted my blind fingertip. I can see nothing but a mottled blueish blur somewhere off Southeast Asia. I forgot I'd need my reading glasses.

'Where has my finger landed, Guy?'

'South China Sea, Pru. D'you think that means the Philippines?'

'No! It doesn't count if my finger lands in water. Spin it again!'

'Use your left hand this time, darling.'

'My left hand? That'll feel awkward. Why should I use my left hand?'

'I don't know. Just a feeling.'

'Right. Here we go!'

Once more I close my eyes. Once more he does the spinning. A tiny trilling. A trilling that slows, stops. I reach out with my left index finger, once more touch the globe's surface, once more open my eyes.

'Mexico,' says Guy.

'Help!'

'Keep your finger steady while I take a closer look at where exactly.'

Guy bends towards the old swollen skin of the globe and peers at it longsightedly.

'Where's it landed, Guysie?'

'A name I don't know, Pwu. I don't know how to say the name. I've no idea what language it is.'

'Really? How's it spelt?'

'O a x a c a.'

'Gosh, that's a very odd name, isn't it?'

'Want to try one more spin?'

'No. We've done enough spinning. Time to pack our bags for – what did you say was the spelling? O a x a c a? How does one get there, Guy? I hope we won't have to go through Los Angeles. All that fuss about so-called *security* they go in for these days at airports in the United States.'

'I've a vague idea one can get to Mexico by way of Santiago or Buenos Aires.'

'Right you are.'

We eye each other up. Guy looks scared. So, I suppose, do I. We know running away takes one nowhere. Bolting, we know, is as bad as balking. One need only ask Jim. A good seat in the saddle, she'd say. A good gait. A good mount, well founded, fitted with the right tackle, blessed with a bit of spirit, answering alertly – warmly – to the reins, the bridle, the spurs, the whip. No need for a new chukka, Jim knows, and Guy knows, and I know. Only the young, or the silly –

Mount Silisili.

Mount Hare.

Only the silly, the simple, or – or seers – think anyone can find meaning in the world by giving up on the world. Yet – I hold out my left hand. My pointing hand. Guy holds out his right hand. We wrap the two hands together. Meagre, his hand feels. Meagre, but wiry. I look into his pallid blue eyes.

'Are we really going to Mexico?' he says. 'Or are we going mad?'

I grin, begin giggling. Giggling so hard I'm soon snorting.

'Troppo, sweetheart. We're going troppo.'

Green Grey Rain

Stevan Eldred-Grigg

Rain on iron rooftops. A radio streaming the latest hit songs. It's the early 1950s. The baby boom. Valarie is a talkative, singing, slanging, pregnant daughter of the slums. Gilbert, her husband, is a well-spoken son of a landed family. They already have three kids. Gilbert has just taken a job as paymaster at a coal mine. The family is about to start life in a green and black and red township on the West Coast.

A little boy is born, almost in a taxi, and named Stevan.

Green Grey rain tells the story of the first years of a little boy dreaming and singing, wondering and wishing, in the bush, rain, rust and sooty streets of 1950s Blackball. A story told by the boy. A story told too by the hit songs he hears on the radio. And a story told by his mother - someone who, with her sister, has already spoken to us in the pages of Oracles and Miracles.

Oracles & Miracles & Zombies

Stevan Eldred-Grigg & Helen Mae Innes

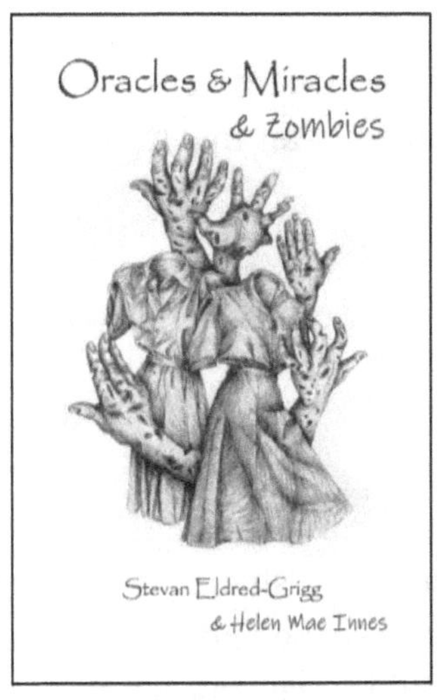

Stevan Eldred-Grigg's best selling novel is back … with zombies!

We all know about the zombie virus that ravaged New Zealand between the two world wars, but little has been written about how the biters it created affected the lives of women, especially working class women. Stevan Eldred-Grigg's best selling novel about twin sisters growing up during the depression has been updated by Helen Mae Innes to include the previously ignored and despised minority, the zombies.

A black comedy, this story shows us how the sisters, their sharp and shrewd mother, and many other women struggled to avoid being bitten by biters, cared gingerly for hunches who didn't want to eat their brains (just yet), and watched as the 'cured' lurkers started to take their jobs.

Even during pandemics girls grow up, worry about boys, go out to work, get married, and have babies, all while trying to keep their brains safe inside their skulls. At the beginning the twins are small, fearful and helpless. By the end of the story they're armed and ready to go after the enemy ... but who is the real enemy?

A novel about survival in extraordinary times, Oracles & Miracles & Zombies is an inspiration to women of all generations.

My History, I think

Stevan Eldred-Grigg

'I am, I suppose, a hoarder. I have carefully filed away all the pain, all the personal shame, that has failed to take written or printed shape and that forms the past. The past, which could break my heart ... ' The year is 1994. A writer lives in a wide white house on a green riverbank. He is writing a book about the lives of rich people a century or so ago. At the same time, he seems to be writing his own story. Neither autobiography nor yet fiction, this fascinating book traces the workings inside the mind of a leading writer. The text twists in and out of the lines of certain stories and novels. We shift from one place to another — from Christchurch to Chicago, from Patagonia to the promenades of Noumea.

Into the Woods

Helen Mae Innes

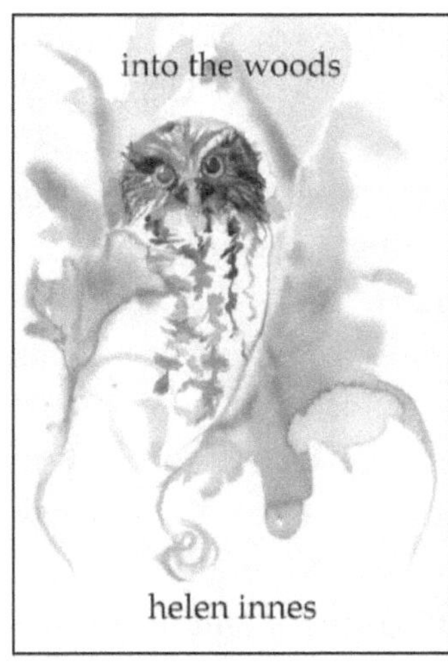

'A funny, painful, powerful story about the strange ways grief moves through us. Helen's path of recovery, from a bed she doesn't want to leave towards a natural world she doesn't know, is full of recognisable difficulties and unlikely connections. This frank and bracing little book has a bass note of personal tragedy but a top note of surprising joy.'

Damien Wilkins

It was during the spring the kaka arrived that I first noticed a grey warbler fledgling outside my window who couldn't get the tune quite right. He'd start singing, get a note wrong and falter, then try tentatively again. Like a child learning the recorder, I thought.

Like a child...

And the Birds Fled to the Bush

Helen Mae Innes

The valley is calm, quiet, waiting. Mrs Henderson thinks it's earthquake weather but she doesn't say anything, doesn't want to make a fuss. It's probably nothing. No one else notices it's quiet, too quiet, until everyone does at the same moment, like at a party when everything goes silent and no one wants to be the first to speak.

All the birds are airborne, and the whole valley holds its breath.

In post-earthquake suburbia everyone is just trying to survive everyday life, eviction by authorities, and infighting between different factions. Meanwhile a specialist in birdsong arrives hoping to conduct research in the surrounding hills. His project is regarded with ire or indifference by all except for Timothy, a weird loner living in the bush, whose speech is odd and behaviour odder.

Making Maths Add Up

Maggie Tu

Maggie's colourful, fun, clear, and mathematically sound approach to teaching maths encourages independent learning and has been peer-reviewed by teachers and students alike. The specialist font makes this resource accessible to all learners.

Instead of teaching fragments of topics artificially divided by the age of the learner Maggie starts at the beginning of each topic and systematically goes through each stage, thereby showing that what is taught over subsequent years in the schooling system can be taught quickly, easily and pain free using this system.

Maggie's book is ideal for both the student who has (allegedly) 'fallen behind' and those who are excelling and are 'ahead' for their year, i.e., all levels can pick up this book, find the stage at which they feel comfortable and start working from there. Students can start at the beginning of each chapter and do the easier exercises quickly as revision or jump straight to the difficult questions.

My Dad

Anneke Gerbrands & Ingrid Kamp

My dad is a beautifully illustrated simple story about a kid and their dad. Its short, simple sentences and use of dyslexia friendly font make it suitable for young readers, but its full-page colourful illustrations also make it attractive to toddlers.

My Dad is written by Anneke Gerbrands and uses New Zealand English making it ideal for dads and kids to read together. Each full page vibrant illustration was lovingly hand drawn by artist Ingrid Kamp.

www.ingramcontent.com/pod-product-compliance
Lightning Source LLC
Chambersburg PA
CBHW032006050726
47590CB00006B/2061